The Mysterious Druids

By Clayton N. Donoghue

FriesenPress

Suite 300 - 990 Fort St
Victoria, BC, V8V 3K2
Canada

www.friesenpress.com

Copyright © 2020 by Clayton N. Donoghue
First Edition — 2020

ISBN
978-1-5255-5643-2 (Hardcover)
978-1-5255-5644-9 (Paperback)
978-1-5255-5645-6 (eBook)

1. HISTORY, EUROPE, GREAT BRITAIN

Distributed to the trade by The Ingram Book Company

Table of Contents

List of Illustrations

Introduction

e regard druids as mysterious simply because we don't understand them. This is not anything new, it can be true about any subject that exists. Once we figure out what it is we are trying to understand, suddenly the mystery disappears. When I first went to college I remember taking a course in mechanical engineering—boy, was it ever mysterious when I first started. The first class was all about the strength and materials in steel. The professor might as well have been speaking in Russian, for absolutely everything he said made no sense to me whatsoever. Since the first assignment was already due in the first week, I had no choice but to stay up late every night going through the text to try to comprehend just exactly what I was expected to do in the assignment. I was extremely tired when I finished, but when I got the mark of seventy percent, I realized I had figured it out.

So, of course, the question might be asked, what does that have to do with anything concerning druids? Well, I more or less used the same procedures in trying to understand the druids as I did in studying mechanical engineering, and

I found the results were much the same. Mind you, this time I did not get a school grade when I figured it out, only a personal satisfaction in coming to feel that there is no mystery to these people after all. That probably takes away all the excitement of the book, and it's likely you want to put it down and try something else. But if you do that you will be disappointed in your action. What the druids represent is an enormous amount of complex knowledge that I think you will be fascinated in learning. That, my friend, is their secret and ultimately their mystery.

Why the druids became a mystery of a shaman-like nature was largely because of politics. They posed a threat to the conventional authorities and what better way to discredit them but to call them witch doctors? Once people hear that term it will quickly turn them off and suddenly the whole subject of druidism is immediately dismissed. That is exactly what happened to the druids, circa 500 AD. When the Christian Church was beginning to make inroads across Western Europe, they were confronted by the druids, particularly in the British Islands. These people proved to be quite intellectual and definitely challenging when it came to arguments. Such was the case when the Christians ran up against a man from Roman Britannia named Pelagius. He was smart and articulate and when the clergy confronted him they were no match for his wit. As the Church was getting a foothold in Britannia it was already being dismantled by just one man. Pelagius had been trained in Brehon law, and he was extremely well versed in it. Brehon law simply says all people are accountable for their own actions and there is no external force that influences you in any of your decisions. This is kind of like the way the law works today. For the Christian Church that challenged their belief in a Divine power that did influence your decisions as was purportedly the case with Joan of Arc.

Since the Church through their best efforts could not successful argue against Pelagius, they quickly resorted to simply calling him a heretic. End of story. Faced with either renouncing his beliefs or being burned at the stake, Pelagius backed down. And when you think about it, who wouldn't? Once the Church realized that a simple threat was all it took to suppress any opposition they were off and running. Suddenly they found they did not have to argue with anybody any more. As for the druids, the clergy went around telling everyone they were shamans and that anyone following them were heretics. If you know your British history, you will thus know Christianity quickly swept the land, and the druids, who had been around for thousands of years, vanished.

Since so little is known of the druids, what I just claimed to be the historical explanation for their disappearance might naturally make some people skeptical. Am I making it all up in defense of the druids? Thus, we come to the heart of the book. I clearly state at the very beginning that the druids were a very complex institution, and so is it true? Were they wiped out due to the Church's political ambitions or were they, in fact, nothing more than an over-glorified bunch of witch doctors? My quick response to that is to take look at Stonehenge. There are numerous experts who say it was engineered by the druids. The math to this construction is nothing short of amazing. Therefore, if the druids did indeed engineer it, then the real truth to their disappearance is that it was, in fact, political.

Mind you, the simplistic design of Stonehenge can be misleading. What you must do is pull out your calculator and figure out the intricacies to the math. Once you do this it will be then that you realize the druids were no shamans. I will discuss this more later, but one of the first people to recognize this in the druids was the Roman historian, Pliny the Elder, in 40 AD. Apparently, he sat down with a druid and discovered the enormous knowledge he had, particularly in mathematics. The fact that none of it had been written down amazed Pliny to no end. Who can do math in their own head? Even today such an ability is an incredible skill. Thus, we know druids were no ordinary people from as far back as the first century. Calling them shamans was in fact a gross misrepresentation of who they really were.

Today many people believe druids are associated only with the Celts. Turns out this is not true at all. Druids are much older than the Celts. They originated with a culture known as the Pan Beaker People at the start of the Bronze Age. This being the case, the druids straddle three major cultural eras; the first one being the Beakers, the second being the Urnfield People, and the final group being the Celts. Each of these cultures is an enormous subject onto itself. Somehow the druids drifted through them with relative ease. I found it would be easier for me to first enlighten the reader on these civilizations before addressing the druids, for it will help reduce the back and forth scenario in telling the story.

When researching the druids, I next found that it would be necessary to explain in detail some of the things they knew. For example, many authors might say something as generic as that druids spent a lot of time watching the skies. My response to that is, so what? Just exactly what was it they were looking at? In this example, I am going to show some of the things they more than likely saw in the sky. What this does is give a clearer picture of some of the things they knew when nobody else did. What we take for granted today was real magic 2000 years ago.

Lastly, I am going to show you the source of their mystery. This may be a bit of a spoiler, but the mystery was more of a manipulation than it was anything else. The whole idea that they possessed some kind of magic power is going to prove to be sheer nonsense. The bottom line on the druids is that they were an extremely intelligent people and nothing more. Their magic was that they knew their stuff and knew how to apply it.

Chapter 1

The Druids And The Neolithic And Bronze Ages

Look at us
Look at you
Their dances write
Our earthbound
Elegy.
We answer
Silently
Our pleasure
Is living
Yours, being.
Who can say
What is right!

Grahaeme B. Young

Under normal circumstances I would have started this chapter with a description of who the druids were, what they looked like, and how they got their name. All of it is pretty typical stuff when it come to the druids, in general. However, I have found that if I go into the norm I will be spending a lot of time going back and forth in history, and after a while I may even confuse myself in trying to explain what it is all about. Therefore, I decided it would be much better to go over some fundamental background first and then introduce the druids later. This way I can simply move forward and continue along that way to the very end.

I came to this way of proceeding when I learned the druids were a lot older than originally thought. It is commonly believed the druids were part of the Celtic culture, since this is where they were last associated. However, I have learned the druids did not start here. A variety of different authors I have read are confident of the real dates when the druids first came into existence. Barry Cunliff, in his book *A Brief History of Druids*, claims the druids started in the fourth century BC. In his book *Druids*, Jean Markale places the starting date for the druids in the eighth century BC. Scholar John Rhys doesn't date when the druids started, but seriously asserts that they predate the arrival of the Celts. In his book *Riddle of the Stones*, Richard Haymond places their beginnings at the time when the stone circles first began to appear. Stone circles in Britain first appeared about 2500 BC. An ancient Greek historian, Hecatius, claimed druids originated around 700 BC. Finally, in *Mythology of the Celtic People*, Charles Squire states that druids originated with the Urnfield People (1500 BC). All of these authors are unanimous in believing that the location where the druids originated was somewhere in northern England. From the archaeological point of view, northern Wales is by far the most popular possibility; specifically, the island of Anglesey.

As always, on the surface it seems straight-forward to say something is a fact until you decide to look just a little bit deeper into the works of these same authors. In this case, we might look in detail at statements made by Strabo, Pliny, and Julius Caesar in what they describe of a druid's appearances. Arch-druids are described as wearing all white and having a flat, gold, moon-shaped disc around their necks. It is implied that the necklace is Celtic. Unfortunately, when you visit the London Museum and the Irish National Museum and see the actual necklaces described, they are dated 2000 – 1500 BC. This is not a Celtic age, but in fact the age of the Bell Beaker People and Tumulus Culture. Suddenly, what seemed very simple has now grown to be very complicated. Now other aspects of the druids have to be examined as well, to see how broad a range of time the druids can actually be found in.

The Bell Beaker People were a culture that inhabited Britain and Ireland from 3000 BC to 1600 BC. This is a particularly interesting group, for not too long ago, back in the 1970s, they were thought interchangeable with the Urnfield People culture. However, due to recent research, the Urnfield People have been declared a group onto themselves. Thus, we now have two groups: Bell Beaker starting in 3000 BC and the Urnfield starting in 1500 BC. A group that straddles them both is the Tumulus People, who have a brief period of 1700 to 1400 BC.

Again, recent research has revealed the Bell Beaker People to be a lot more advanced than originally thought. Apparently, their metallurgy was one of their defining features. They had advanced skills in working with copper and gold. It is from them that the famous, gold, half-moon necklace disk originated. I can remember that for the longest time this item was considered Celtic. As can be seen, science has come a long way in such a short time. The Bell Beaker People's origins are not fully understood but it is thought they were from somewhere in northern Europe stretching from Denmark to the mouth of the Seine River. Of course, how they got their name was from the extensive research done into their pottery designs, much of which looks like upside-down bells. Next, is the shape and design of their homes; they were rectangular. Further, Michael Parker Pearson discovered that these structures were much further ahead in building practice than were those of the Celts. The Bell Beaker People used wooden dowels to secure the frame. This is a technique that does not appear again until the Iron Age. On one site, a glass tube was uncovered, which had likely been made in Syria. This showed these people had trade that went as far as the Mediterranean; something that is a very new idea to archaeologists. Then, of course, in a site in Scotland was found the earliest form of a weaving loom, which verified they did not just walk around in animal skins—they knew how to make clothes. Thousands of flint arrowheads more than confirmed they had developed the bow for hunting. Lastly, and by far the most inspiring of all their achievements—these were the people who built Stonehenge. I will get into more detail about this later.

Beaker People Pottery

The next civilization after the Beaker People was the Tumulus Culture People, another recent discovery. As archaeology continues to dig up finds, the more evidence there is to compare one culture with another, or in this case to discover a whole new culture. For the longest time the sequence of Neolithic cultures were first the Bell Beaker People, followed by the Urnfield People. The Tumulus culture was first determined in Germany, circa 2000. Two things distinguished them. The first one was their type of burials and the second was their design in pottery. A Tumulus burial site is distinct. It's a small round hill with a stone wall and it is only big enough to hold one person. They are not as spread out as a Bell Beaker hill is. The pottery has a distinct, funnel-like top with a perfect round bulb, which has groups of three lateral-line groove designs that go from the top of the pot all the way to the bottom. Archaeologists have only recently determined the origins of the culture is along the Elbe river from Belgium to Bavaria.

Like the Urnfield People the Tumulus People migrated west and consumed the whole of Western Europe.

Tumulus Pottery

Based on the time frame it is more than likely it was the Bells Beaker People who built Stonehenge and Newgrange. As many know, these two colossal sites were a feat of amazing engineering. Both sites are known to have all sorts of religious and solar aspects and it is from them that we come across our first eyewitness account that druids were seen practicing their rituals here. The person who first witnessed what he clearly identified as druids was Hecataeus of Abdera (Greece). He wrote a document called *Hibernians*. Unfortunately, there is not much of the document left, but there's enough of it that we do get an idea of who he is talking about.

Another person in more contemporary times was John Aubrey, who in 1660 associated the druids with the stone circles. He wrote an unpublished book, *Monumenta Britannica*, in which he includes a first-hand account that the druids were still practicing their arts in Avebury stone circles. John Aubrey is the person who discovered the famous Aubrey post holes at Stonehenge. In his writings he is emphatic that the stone circles were engineered by the druids. Later, as many will know, the famous William Stukeley makes the same observation in his studies of the stone circles. From both men come numerous references as proof druids were heavily involved with the stone circles. Again, I will get more into this subject later, for now I am simply trying to put many of the pieces together to establish the oldest time frame the druids could possibly have lived in. If Stonehenge and Newgrange are in fact connected with druid activities, then it puts their time line as far back as 2500 BC. When I get to the subject of Stonehenge there will be rather overwhelming evidence this claim is credible.

Moving on, the next culture to emerge in time is the Urnfield People, who date from 1200 BC to 350 BC. We are still learning new things from them all the time. For example, up until just recently it was believed the Urnfield People originated in Denmark and made their way across Western Europe. Now discoveries are showing they may have actually originated in Hungary before migrating into Western Europe. The date at which they started is also now coming into question. A few years back, scholars were very confident in saying the Urnfield began circa 2500 BC.

Since most literature and research has the Urnfield as the people who spent most of the time in Britain prior to the arrival of the Celts it seems they should get most of the credit for the cultural developments of the druids. If we accept the time frame for when the druids originated from writers like Jean Markale, then there is no question that the Urnfield culture was the primary period they came from.

The Celts are definitely a long way off from being the origin of the druids.

Now that we have established that the druids were likely from the Urnfield People period, another fact has to be established as well, and that is what age this was in. The correct age makes a huge impact for it tells us what advancements were already in existence when the druids first emerged. British archaeologists say the Bronze Age started somewhere around 1500 BC in Britain, but it was painfully slow getting going. Therefore, if we are to agree the druids came into existence around 800 BC, then we know it was when the Bronze Age was fully developed. Seeing a bronze sword, for example, would have been a near-common sight. What this says about the druids is they were in an advanced technological period. In her book *Exploring the World of the Druids,* Miranda Green has found that much of the physical evidence connected to druids, like their bronze divination saucer, is squarely dated to the Bronze Age. Also, the famous small, crystal-glass ball that druids carried is dated to 500 BC from Syria. Palmyra was the biggest exporter of the finest glass in the Bronze Age Mediterranean world. Thus, from these artifacts we find verification that the druids were indeed primarily from this time frame.

There is an overlap of terms due to the fact that scholars and historians are overly generous with the words "Age" and "Period," and some explanation is needed to clarify things just a bit. There were two great Ages in our past. One is called the Neolithic Age (time frame 3000 BC to 2000 BC). It was followed by the Bronze Age (time frame 1800 BC to 500 BC). It was followed by yet another Age known as the Iron Age (time frame 500 BC to AD 300). Within these ages are cultural development periods of civilizations. As I have pointed out, the first one was the Bell Beaker People period (time frame 2000 BC to 1600 BC). They were followed by the Tumulus Culture Period (time frame 1600 BC to 1300 BC). Next, came the Urnfield People Period). As you can see, the periods of culture are within the ages of overall characteristics. Unfortunately, I have found with British and Danish historical authorities in particular that they interchange the ages with the cultural group periods and it makes it very confusing. I have even seen Michael Parker Pearson jumble up the terms when he should know better. Often, they simply cluster the cultural groups (Beaker, Tumulus, and Urnfield) into one age. Where it gets confusing is when they describe specifics such as the pottery that's been found. They say bizarre things such as a pot that has been found at a certain site has changed in design through time. The implications are that the pottery found in the same location originated from the same people when, in fact, this is anything but the case. I found the same two groups (British and Danish) do this even more when it comes to the arrival of the Celts (350 BC). They have a great deal of difficulty correctly identifying this culture, so they simply call them Iron Age people. This can be proved as completely incorrect when they start going into specifics, like identifying cultural achievements, weapons, habitats, and clothing. It has to be remembered the Romans and Greeks were also in the Iron Age, but no one ever calls them Iron Age People.

Now to quickly show the difference in the three big Ages; Neolithic, Bronze, and Iron. The Neolithic Period is generally recognized as a time when mankind overall operated with stone and wood. Everything is typically described in generic terms. People were, for the most part, hunters and gatherers. There was not much farming going on, so there were no specific boundaries of specific groups and activities. In terms of technology, recent research now shows that it was a lot more complicated than previously thought. The homes built in this age were not just huts such as those you might have seen with some of the North American natives. In Britain they have actually found evidence of well-built, sturdy houses. Of course, Stonehenge has unraveled the whole archaeological community in general. How was it built in a time when there was no real infrastructure for a bureaucratic civilization? In general terms, the Neolithic people were recognized as a hunter-gatherer society. Life expectancy was very short and superstition very high. Lastly, communication was all oral; written or hieroglyphic communication had not yet come about.

The next age was the Bronze Age. This is when weapons like swords and shields start appearing. For the first-time, mankind has the ability to forge metal. Also, for the first-time recognizable forts and garrisons start to pop up everywhere. Forms of organized nations are coming into their own and in some cases a written language is seen. The hunting and gathering age is ending and growing crops and owning property is now in place. With the ownership of property comes the instinct to protect it from outsiders. Thus, we have communities who organize themselves into armed bodies to fend off unwelcome guests. Where in the Neolithic Age the primary line of thinking was devoted to worship of ancestors, new elements are added with domestic issues of defense. Religion begins to dwindle in daily importance. The huge stone circles are gradually being abandoned. Using the new tools from this time frame, mankind starts two great civilizations, Mesopotamia and

Egypt, where the world's first bureaucracies come into existence. The world of nations is born. By the late Bronze Age even more nations start to appear like Greece, Etrusca, and the Hittites. In southern Europe begins the foundation of a people who will eventually sweep the entire continent—the Celts. They start up in the mountains known as Halstatt and at this stage they are a mixture of three cultures; Scythian, Doric, and German. Though they begin at a crude level of development they mature fast. By 400 BC they have their first major migration into western Europe. The thing to note with this first group is that there no evidence of druids amongst them. Their leading cultural aspect is Scythian and Germanic.

Finally, we have the Great Iron Age. As mentioned it does not reach central Europe until around 500 BC. It becomes one of the biggest oddities of history because historians emphatically claim that primitive cultures are living side by side with advanced cultures with absolutely no intersection. Here I am compelled to completely agree with archaeologist Francis Pryor and historian Peter Clayton in *Archaeological Sites of Britain*, by saying this is complete rubbish! The early Roman Republic was nowhere near as technically advanced as many writers would have you believe. Their greatness came as a result of sharing, incorporating, and adapting to all the surrounding cultures they ended up conquering. By this point in time there were dozens of new cultures all over central Asia, the Mediterranean, and Europe, like Carthage, Minoa, Palestine, Gaul, Persia, Briton, Iberia, Germania, and Thracia. In these cultures we know there was written language; the start of world trade; governments; and organized, armed conflicts. The Celts were not as advanced politically as the Romans were, but they had far more advanced knowledge in metals than the Romans did. The Greeks were superior in art and building and the Syrians were still the best makers of glass. Pryor and Clayton share the opinion that the world was simply a case of one big over-lapping community. It is from that point we probably can now have the best understanding of the druids. If they survived over the millennia as now seems to be the case, then they adapted to their ever-changing world.

CHAPTER 2

The Druids and the Celts

They are of great strength
They are of great passion
They are of great emotion
They are of great sadness
And
They are of great loyalty

"CELTS" – GREEK – UNKNOWN – FIFTH CENTURY

S ince the Celts are the biggest association to the druids it only seems natural they should be addressed next. I know it must seem strange I am still discussing the ancient world and that I have not formally introduced what a druid is, but you will later see that it will be much easier approach it this way than in the standard format; druid first and then their traits.

The Celts

Previously I made mention that when the Celts started to appear in Europe, many scholars did not recognize them to be a distinct culture. Now you will see they were a discrete people and along with the druids, they did have an impact.

Circa 800 BC, three major cultural groups came together in the hills of modern-day Austria in a place called Halstatt. They did not have a name for themselves and research shows that as the succeeding generation carried on from the nucleus, they never made any references to themselves as a nation either. When they first came in contact with these strange people wearing pants, it was the Greeks who first addressed them as Keltaes. This got abbreviated to Kelt and now today, Celts.

Since this first group started at Halstatt, scholars decided to call them Halstatt Celts. The Celts later went through another evolution and moved from Austria to Switzerland. This group of Celts became known as La Tène Celts. Again, the name came from the place in which they primarily resided. The Halstatt Celts merged together with three other peoples and matured into "Celts" around 400 BC. The famous Hochdorf burial in the lower, south-western corner of Germany is where archaeologists say that the Celts truly melded into one society. The artifacts found in the Hochdorf burial clearly show that these three-major cultures at last joined into one.

The next aspect of the Halstatt was that they had a distinct language, which has now come to be recognized as Goidelic Gaelic. The remnants of the language have survived in modern-day Irish and Scottish. The La Tène Celts matured as an entity on to themselves around 250 BC. Like their predecessors they too went on a major migration that swept most of Western Europe as far as Britain, but not Ireland, and into Eastern Europe and as far as modern-day Turkey. The archaeological finds in La Tène, Switzerland itself are how scholars were able to see that this group of Celts was uniquely different from its predecessors. However, it should be noted that despite the changes these people are still regarded as Celts and nothing else. The La Tène Celts developed their very own serious art form. Their advanced skill in weapon making was admired by Julius Caesar. They also developed a new form of Gaelic called Brythonic. The language survives in modern-day Welsh and Cornish.

It is a natural curiosity that since the two groups of Celts didn't even speak the same language how it is that they are still recognized as Celts. The answer is that their outward appearance, behavior, and customs were very similar to each other. The biggest example was their pants with the plaid design on them—that did not change. They were the only people in all the known world to be wearing pants—it was a unique trait. This aspect of their appearance was accompanied by their hairstyles and facial hair. Celts wore their hair long with a droopy horseshoe mustache. It was the signature appearance for all Celts and both Halstatt and La Tène maintained it. Also, in terms of clothing, both Celtic cultures wore the same woolen plaid cape, which was secured with a beautifully designed brooch. This is how the scholars are able to say that the two groups of Celts were the same people.

The areas where they differed were in the language, politics, art forms, foods, and metallurgy.

The Halstatt Celts spoke a rough, guttural language known as Goidelic. Their politics were very similar to the Mediterranean kingship system. However, what was unique to this group was that their kings were elected, not born into the position. One of the leading food items that clearly separated them from the later La Tène Celts was wine, which was a major part of their diet. Next, their art forms, though unique, had a lot of Thracian influence in them. Their weapons included the long, teardrop, cast-iron swords, which had the same metal composition as all the weapons of the time.

The La Tène Celts' biggest distinction is more their politics than anything else. They developed what has been recognized as a warrior class society. Like their predecessors, their leaders were elected, but were no longer crowned king. They were more chairpersons than anything. What kept them in office was their fighting ability. To a certain extent what happened with Vortigern in Wales after the Romans left in AD 410 is an example of the system. Even though it was something of a case of him seizing power, he never crowned himself king. From his perspective he followed the La Tène style of politics. When he failed to contain the Saxons, he soon forcibly took over Vortimer.

Moving on in terms of culture, the La Tène Celts really perfected their art forms and the best example of this can be found in the *Book of Kells* and the *Lindisfarne Gospels*. In terms of food, mead is definitely the signature change in the diet. Wine was now only a privileged-class drink. The common person didn't bother with it anymore. Lastly, the metallurgy skills had dramatically improved with the La Tène Celts. Cast-metal swords were replaced with well-made, folded metal swords.

What you've just read are the overall differences between the two major societies. In the areas of worship there is also a difference, but the changes happened when the migrations began, and the Celts were exposed to the cultures they assimilated. From the research Amanda Green has done on Celt religion, she feels the Halstatt Celts had many of the same attributes of the Etruscan and Greek cultures. However, this quickly changed once they were exposed to the Urnfield People. Burials, for example, were brief and non-ceremonious when the Celts were stationed in Austria. It was felt the Scythian aspect had the biggest influence on the Celts, since they were a mobile culture. However, once exposed to the Urnfield they kept to their brief burial practices but started burying their dead near their homes. Their belief in the pagan gods followed the same principles as the Mediterranean practices.

When it came to gods, the La Tène Celts developed a whole new series of their own and became completely independent. Gods like Cernonus, Lugh, Brigid, Dagda, Morrigan, and Epona, started to come into existence, just to mention a few. However, there was a unique twist in that the Celts didn't necessarily worship these gods but saw them as representatives of nature. I will get more into this later, but it is a real departure from the normal way of how pagan religion operated. Both the La Tène and the Halstatt Celts began adopting the principle of worshiping their ancestors. I would say the special festivals like Samhain came about with the La Tène Celts, since they are so widely recognized as being the founders of it, but that would be untrue. The special festivals such as Beltaine, Samhain, Lughnasah, and Imbolc came from an earlier time. In terms of burial practices, the La Tène adopted some and had a few of their own. Burying in mounds and groves is a custom taken from the Urnfield. Archaeologists have found a mixed bag of practices took place where in some cases the body was buried whole, and in others the body was cremated. In other words, there is no set signature of the La Tène Celt burial pattern. This is what separates their practices from the Halstatt Celts.

CHAPTER 3

Druid Society

If trees need any measurement,
Then let it be by metaphor.
A two-man saw can cut one down
And standing there with tacky hands,
You only know how old it was.
What years were lean or otherwise.
No reason for a seed at all.
No, metaphor's the thing for trees.

STEVEN WILSON-FLOYD

ow that we have established the various types of cultures and the ages the druids lived in, we can concentrate on describing who they were. You will appreciate that there will be no stopping and starting in explaining the world the druids were living in—you already know it.

Thus, we can now begin.

The word druid: From what can be understood, the name was first thought of as being Greek but was later seen as ancient Latin—definitely not Gaelic. It means "knowledge of oak." This in turn has been expanded to mean "oak teacher." I know it's not Gaelic because in Gaelic the word for oak is "bot." Goes to show that when too many people get involved with a subject it can quickly get confusing. As always, the title is what the Romans and Greeks called the people walking around in white robes, but the druids did not call themselves this until after Julius Caesar came to Gaul in 55 BC. It is not known what the druids called themselves, but seeing that trees appeared to be their primary focus in everything they did, chances are the title they gave themselves involved trees in some way. In many of their ceremonies the oak tree was extremely important, which is how they became identified with it.

In the first chapter I presented numerous sources who identified the druids with a large assortment of skills and showed that we can safely say it is not unreasonable to suggest they came into existence around 2500 BC in Bronze Age Britain. This statement clearly implies the druids had a hand in the making of Stonehenge and Newgrange. This, by the way, is not a new idea. The first person to come up with it was William Stukeley in the eighteenth century. He was the first person to seriously examine the great stone circle.

There are enormous amounts of documentation on the appearance of druids. They wore white robes much like medieval monks did. They used a leather belt, which held up a leather pouch. Their hair was cut back halfway and called a tonsure. If he was an arch-druid or *sacerdotal* to a king, he would have a gold disc on his head and a gold torc around his neck. Finally, he had a walking cane, made of either willow or oak. Apparently, there was a reasonable explanation for this; both kinds of wood preserved well against the elements. It from this we get our first glimpse into their association to trees. It is widely accepted they had a commanding knowledge of just about all the known trees. The divination practice of Ogham is centred on the magic of trees. I will be getting into this in more detail later.

The druidic order was very extensive and there were other types of druids, who were for the most part recognized by the colour of their robes. The next highest-ranking druid was known as a vate or an ovate (both names are in common use). He also wore white but did not wear a gold headpiece; so as Julius Caesar quickly found out, he could be easily confused with an arch-druid. The vates were the ones who conducted religious ceremonies in the forest groves and the stone circles. They had all the same authority as the arch-druids but could not counsel a king. The next druid was the bard. In training, the bard was actually quite low in schooling. At best he may have been trained for five years to master his craft. However, in a royal court he had a lot of authority, as was the case of Torne in the stories around Niall of the Nine Hostages. From what I could find out about it, a bard wore a blue robe or a white one with some coloured markings either on the sleeve or collar. Apparently, bards were taught music by the use of colours. After them, came the brehons. I have not been able to find a definitive colour marking for them, but they must have had one; for a brehon was said to be easily recognized at a glance. One source claims they had either a grey robe or a white robe with black markings on the sleeves. A brehon was in training for over ten years, mastering the laws of the land. They were a mix of lawyer and judge at the same time. After this, there were three more kinds of druids, who had specialized skills; physicians, historians, and craft experts. It due to the craft experts that scholars feel the druids had the capability to build Stonehenge. In *21 Lessons of Merlyn*, Douglas Monroe claims the druids had a commanding knowledge of engineering. I found out he got this information from the Roman writer, Pliny the Elder. Again, each of these druids was easily recognized by the colour scheme of his costume.

The education of the druids is another well documented aspect of the institution. I have several sources on this one; Jean Markale, Amanda Green, Douglas Monroe, and Brendan Cathbad Myers (*The Mysteries of Druidry*). To achieve the rank of a white-robe druid it took twenty-one years of study and memorization. It was a rule that nothing was to be written down. Everything learned was through memorization. From the populous, druids selected children who showed an exceptional ability to learn. Not just any one could become a druid. When you see the type of training they went through it is understandable. You basically had to have a photographic memory in order to get through it all. According to Douglas Monroe, there is a book called *The Pheryllt*, which is claimed to be the most complete study on all the training of druids. Of course, the natural criticism of this is, if nothing was allowed to be written down, how did this book come to be written? I had to go check with other sources to verify just how much of my story was correct and I found a few but not many. Therefore, you should be cautioned on how much to believe of this next part.

The druid training was broken down into parts. The first level was simple exercises and memorizations of what are called axioms; small bardic poems. The new student would get one each day and was expected to know it by the end of the day. Every day he was tested to see if he/she remembered it. By the end of the year, the student was expected to be able to recite all 365 axioms. On this point I found there is some validity, for it is well recognized that on festival Samhain (November 1st) a similar practice was conducted with the brehons (druid lawyers). They had to recite all the laws of the land to the king, so he knew what authority he actually had. The first level of exercise was simply a test to see if the student had the capability to memorize a vast amount of knowledge.

After that initiation, it would appear the training breaks down into four five-year cycles, plus an initiation year. The initiation year was to see if the young student could do the training and be trusted with the knowledge. This accounts for how it all adds up to a training of twenty-one years. The first level of training is bardic (poets /musicians). The second is brehon. The third is historic and medical, and the fourth is astronomy and religion. I found it very interesting that the bardic level was very low on the scale of learning yet was ranked very high politically. A bard in a Celtic court wielded a lot of influence with a king. If you are familiar with the famous Drumceat Council in 575 AD Ireland, you will know that all the high-level druids were dismissed from the Irish courts except for the bards. A bard was given a special medallion, so he had complete freedom to wander the entire kingdom without interference. Two great names that show proof of this are Taliesin of Britain and Oisin of Ireland. Bards might be compared to our modern rock stars. They had an enormous amount of influence in society. It is also interesting that brehon does not rank as high as a historian. You have to go to Welsh records to know the reason for this.

In Wales, where Vortigern had dismissed the druids in AD 425, disputes over his legitimacy as king were an ongoing problem. What later became the reading of the chronicles at a coronation had once been the duty of a historian druid to recite the pedigree of leadership. This was a huge responsibility. Screw this up and it would likely end your life. Therefore, a historian ranked very high.

We are now at the first stage of powerful responsibility and the druids knew it. At this same stage, the student druid now also learned the arts of healing. According to the *Pheryllt* there was a huge series of lessons on learning all the different herbs and medicines for healing people. Being a physician was as serious then as it today. Helping the sick and injured had to be exact and the druids were well aware of it. Though the church dismissed druids as shamans we find here it was nowhere near the case. Especially with the Celts you have to remember they were ferocious fighters and it did not take much to upset them. To find that a druid was a phony when it came to medicine was extremely dangerous.

Lastly, we have astronomy and religion. As you can see, the highest order was devoted to the gods. In Julius Caesar's Gaulic Campaign notes, he sees better than anyone how the druids could spellbind the Celts into doing anything they wanted via their pagan religion. The druids knew this only too well and therefore, above all else, the stability of a tribe or nation was dependant upon making the right call.

This is how the education process worked. And remember, it was done through memorization. Further, each student had to swear an oath never to reveal the druidic secrets to anyone including family members.

Where they trained, who they trained, and how they trained, has always been one of the big curiosities of the druids. On this I had to rely heavily on Douglas Monroe and Jean Markale for the answers. Since the training was so heavily guarded, it was mostly done on a one-to-one basis though there were occasions where one druid took on two students. In the writings about Vercingetorix, this seems to have been the case. Vercingetorix's druid master took him and a female as students. She turned out to become an exceptional warrior druid. The school, so-to-speak, was everywhere. Druid and student would travel the length of the country but on special occasions go to places where special festivals like Samhain were going on. In Ireland that would have been at Tara. Britain, according to the archaeologist Francis Pryor Maiden Castle, was said to be the most popular place to travel. The evidence from The _Book of Pheryllt_ indicates that the reason for the extensive traveling was because the particular subject was in different parts of the country. For example, if the student was at the level of astronomy, it is very obvious he would be taken to Knowth in Ireland and Stonehenge in Britain. The Isle of Man has numerous mythological references about this being the place to go to study martial arts. That the druids traveled the length of the Celtic world is heavily recorded by ancient Greek and Roman writers such as Strabo and Pliny. Thus, it is not farfetched that the training of a druid took on this method.

There were a number of places that had particular reputations with druids but by far the most famous was Anglesey in Wales. You might say it was the Vatican of the druid world. Julius Caesar writes a lot about the special religious sanctuary in Briton. In AD 60, the Roman general, Seutonius Paullinus, sacked the place as being his highest priority to eliminate the druid threat to the Roman Empire. In Ireland, Tara is also well documented as another major centre for druids. In Gaul, Marseille was a major druid centre and again the Romans completely destroyed it. After this, there was a series of minor druid centres for special gatherings; Emain Macha in Ulster, Iona in Scotland, the Man-on-ton stone in Cornwall, and of course Stonehenge and Newgrange. Then when we get into the herbs and trees we know the druids would have taken the student to where certain plant life was in abundance. By the time a druid was fully trained he would have done some serious touring of the continent of Europe.

When at last the apprentice was a fully trained druid, it was expected some form of office was assigned him/her. From the documents written about the Irish king Cormac McAirte in AD 261, everyone realized the druids controlled nearly all aspects of life. Julius Caesar in particular noticed that point, for the political power of the druids was enormous. When health, politics, culture, and religion were all in their domain it's not hard to understand how they ended up being the centre of the community. In the Irish annals it's mentioned numerous times that the king could not speak or make a formal announcement until he'd first consulted with his arch-druid. When you review the history of Ireland in the *Book of the Four Masters,* you see the druids provided a degree of political stability. After Drumceat everything began to fall apart. Basically, the country fell into civil war that lasted for close to a hundred years on and off. So, eliminating their druids was not a smart move.

The sinister side of druids is what a lot of people are curious about, simply to verify they were, in fact, an evil institution and really should have been stamped out. Once again, there is not much evidence to prove any of these claims from an archaeological position. There are only three examples in Europe so far that appear to support that druids (vates) were engaged in human sacrifice. One is found in Denmark (the Tollund Man), one in Britain (the Lindow Man), and one in Ireland (the Clonycavan Man). All are dated to around 2000 BC. What I find interesting about accusing the druids of these atrocities is that it's one more way to date how far back the druids actually go. The point here is that if you are going say the druids were responsible for these atrocities, then you are also going to have to accept their date of origin goes back to these dates as well. These are the kinds of things I keep note of when people say druids only officially go back to the Celts and yet in the same breath say the druids were involved in human sacrifices. Anyway, if I am to concede that the druids did partake in such gruesome activities, as can be seen in these three bodies, it hardly constitutes mass killing by the druids. As Jean Markale and Barry Cunliffe (*Brief History of the Druids*) point out, when you compare it to the killings by the Romans in the colosseums, it makes the druids look like Boy Scouts.

Naturally, the biggest question about druids that I have heard time and again is, did the druids actually have any magical powers in the manner of Merlyn? The answer is a flat no! I know for some this must be disappointing, for so much legend has arisen over this and the curiosity is overwhelming. Unfortunately, the secret doesn't lie in the fantasy stories in such books as *Dun Cow of Clonmacnoise,* but in the druids extreme patience in observing all things around them. From everything I have gathered about them, they come off more like university professors than magicians. One of the first persons to note this quality in the druids was Pliny the Elder, of Rome. He wrote extensively about druids and admired their intellect. I assume from the writings he had first-hand experience of them. Since much of what he wrote does check out, the observation may be correct. Since his time and all the way up to William Stukeley, all the people who do in-depth research on the druids come up with the same conclusion; the druids were remarkably well-educated people. Hardly an image the church wanted the public to have. When I start to get into some of the specifics of their practices you will see first-hand how keen this observation is. This kind of approach helps to explain a lot when it comes to how the druids survived through the centuries.

The Bell Beaker People and the Urnfield People were, by and large, domestic, non-militaristic people. The Celts, on the other hand, were extremely violent. No doubt with the Celts' arrival into Western Europe the druids knew they had to adapt to this aggressive culture or they would too disappear. What is interesting is that they managed to preserve a number of their customs from the previous period going into the age of the Celts. The biggest example, which I will explain in more detail later, is the lunar cycle and the four major Celtic festivals; Samhain, Lughnasah, Imbolc, and Beltane. These are not Celtic festivals but in fact began with the Bell Beaker People. The authority on this observation is Michael Parker Pearson from his extensive research at Stonehenge in 2005. The people of Britain circa 2500 BC celebrated the seasons from a practical perspective as a reminder of the activities they should be engaged in for their own preservation. Once the Celts swept the whole of Western Europe and there was nothing left to pillage, they were stuck with the problem of what to do next. Seems the druids came out and explained to them that their survival depended on the environment itself, such as growing crops and raising livestock. The nomadic nature of the Celts now began to change to be more domestic. And so, in order for the Celts to remember what they should be doing at certain times of the year, the festivals helped them along. Just as two examples, Beltane was for planting crops and Lughnasah was for harvesting.

Now that I have mentioned the fact people believe that druids were some kind of mystical people, it cannot be ignored they did practice the art of divination. However, as pointed out by both Amanda Green and Peter B. Ellis (*The Druids*) it has all been played way out of proportion in modern marketing. You can find books by the hundred now on Ogham, Celtic Animal Oracles, and Celtic Tara Cards in just about every bookstore throughout Europe and North America. From that alone you can get the impression the druids must have been obsessed with casting spells on everybody. Nothing could be further from the truth. Here's when you actually have to sit down and read some of the many thousands of stories on the druids in folklore histories of Britain, Ireland, Wales, and Scotland. If you take, for example, the legendary Irish story of Deirdre and Naoise, you will learn that in this beautiful, tragic tale the druid Cathbad only cast one divination in the whole story. The same is true in the great story of the Táin Bó Cuailnge. Queen Maeve asks her druid to make a divination on the upcoming campaign, and again, this is the only time it happens in the entire story. From the research I did into this stuff, I found the instructions on the fortune-telling packages clearly state divination was not be used very often, clearly implying it was used sparingly. Druids also had a crystal ball they carried, but to date I have only found one reference on how they used it, meaning its use was far less prevalent than Hollywood would have us believe.

The reason is that druids were very careful at everything they did. They were fully aware of how potentially dangerous it could be, especially when dealing with the volatile Celts. The stories of Celt savagery are too many to count. The slightest provocation would be grounds enough for your head to be cut off. Also, for simple common sense, you don't want to over-do it. Amanda Green and Julius Caesar did seem to agree on one point; the druids wanted to be seen as mysterious. To portray this image things had to be done sparingly. Each act or decision had to be seen as a special occasion. Julius Caesar wrote that he once witnessed a druid walk onto a battlefield and by raising his hands in a magical way prevented two Celtic armies from clashing. It was something straight out of the movie *Lord of the Rings*. Most of the activities in the daily life of a druid were in studying.

Since Caesar made such a fuss over druid political influence, I figure I will comment on just exactly how much influence they really had. It is true druids had an extremely high rank in Celtic society. The same was true with the Beaker People and the Urnfield People. Druids did not pay taxes and were not required to do military service when the king called men to arms. They were free to travel between kingdoms and could travel abroad as well. This point is documented by Strabo and Diadoros of ancient Greece. The vates controlled all religious ceremonies including funerals and sacrifices. As mentioned, divinations were one of their central tools of control. Normally, to control a king the method was they would put a geis on him when he first took office. A geis is kind of a hex, you might say. Kings were prevented from doing a certain act under a geis and if they broke this rule, it automatically meant they were removed from office. Druids, for obvious reasons, were very watchful that the kings not violate a geis and the kings were aware of it. Thus, the druid had a special power over the king just in this one aspect. The next step came only too easy for a druid in that a king could not make any announcement without speaking to his druid first. On that point you have to remember all the laws were controlled by the brehons. On Samhain, the laws were reviewed and if required new ones were implemented. Kings were naturally subject to the law. There was no such thing as Divine authority as was the case in British history during the Tudor period. It comes as no surprise that if the king was subject to the will of the druid, then so was everyone else. Crossing a druid was unthinkable.

When Christianity arrived, the power of the druids began to wane. Kings were told druids were evil and that they should be gotten rid of, and starting in the fifth century druids began to slowly disappear. This is an ominous point in the stories of King Arthur, when the old Celtic ways were being abandoned. When you consider that the druids controlled all the cultural aspects of the Celts, then the Celts were disappearing with them. Today, scholars are having a tremendous challenge in trying to identify just how much culture was lost due to the termination of the druids. One of the areas where a real measurement can made as to druid influence was in their music and art, expressed through the bards. Various claims have been made that the average bard knew hundreds of poems. Definitely that knowledge no longer exists today. Again, the famous Convention of Druim Cett (Drumceat) in Ulster in AD 575 was a major turning point. The council was originally designed to settle a dispute between the King of Ulster and Dal Riata, but the druids were dragged into it as well. Whatever control the druids still had was formally removed. In Briton (or the former Roman Britannia) when Vortigern came to power, he simply dismissed them from all real power. From that point on, druids were relegated to the supervision of ceremonial events only. They were no longer seen in royal courts. In Ireland violence erupted between the various kingdoms on a level not seen ever before. As such it seriously weakened them when the foreign invaders arrived like the Anglo-Saxons, the Vikings and Normans.

CHAPTER 4

Famous Druids

O Merlin in your crystal cave
Deep in the diamond of the day,
Will there ever be a singer
Whose music will smooth away
The furrow drawn by Adam's finger
Across the memory and the wave?
Or a runner who'll outrun
Man's long shadow driving on,
Break through the gate of memory
And hang the apple on the tree?
Will your magic ever show
The sleeping bride shut in her bower,
The day wreathed in its mound of snow
and Time locked in his tower?

EDWIN MUIR

ne of the big things I have noticed about books written about druids in the past is that they depict druids as a faceless people. They're shown as some mysterious race that has no personal identity and allows the general public to imagine them as far more magical than they really were. You've already seen from what I have written so far that most of their magic was simply that they knew things about their surroundings that most other people weren't bothered to learn. The alleged magic they had was conjured up more out of superstition than real fact. What I thought I would do here is give a number of examples of who some of the druids were and what they became famous for. Though many are fictitious, this introduction to some of them helps us to realize they were human and that what they did was, for the most part, very down to earth and practical.

Probably the best druid to start off with is Cathbad of Ulster. He is considered to be semi-real on account of his time frame being accurate. There is also a strong possibility that the king he served under, King Conchobar (Connor) McNessa, was a real historical figure. Since both people were in the time of the legendary character the great Cu Chulainn, from the famous story the *Tain Bo Cuailnge*, officially Cathbad is still a fictional person. Yet this story is one of our great close looks at what druids were and what influence they really had. *Tain Bo Cuailnge*, along with another story about Dierdre and Macha, is part of a bigger story group known as the Ulster Cycle. These stories are dated together in the first century of Ireland.

Cathbad makes his big entrance when asked by King Conchobar to make a divination upon a newly-born baby girl. She is very adorable, and it appears she will grow up to be equally beautiful, which she does. Her name is Deirdre. Since she is of royal blood it doesn't take Cathbad to realize she will draw the interest of many a prince when she becomes a gorgeous princess. The violent character of Celts likely will be the cause of many a lustful feud. Therefore, Cathbad predicts the child will be the cause of bloody in-fighting and that many will lose their lives because of her. This causes quite a stir amongst the nobles and they demand she be put to death right away. Conchobar intercedes and claims her for his own, but when Deirdre grows up, she wants nothing to do with the aging king. Instead, she chooses a young warrior by the name Naios and they elope to Scotland. The king bides his time and manages to seduce the couple to come back to Ulster. No sooner are they on Irish soil when he has his warriors go after Naios. Eventually they kill him but not until hundreds die in the process. Conchobar at last has his prize but not her heart and in the end, Deirdre takes her own life and Ulster ends exactly as Cathbad had predicted, in complete ruin.

What can be readily seen is there is no magic as is depicted in the tales of King Arthur. Cathbad is a down-to-earth, pragmatic person. In this story and many more after it Cathbad always gives the often-chaotic king a sensible judgement, and when the king screws up, as he always does, Cathbad is there to say, "I told you so." If anything, Cathbad shows probably the most positive and sensible side of druids. He is never seen in a dungeon somewhere making up magical potions to enchant people with as in Hollywood movies. He is exactly what Julius Caesar portrayed; someone at the king's side providing reason for sound judgement. I am sure had King Conchobar asked

Cathbad what he should do with Deirdre, Cathbad would have likely have come up with an acceptable solution, however, this would have deprived Ireland of one of the country's most romantic stories.

In Ireland another well-known mythological druid is Amergin Glu'igel. He is not as famous as Cathbad, but he is ranked pretty high in the order of things. His claim to fame is that he led the Milesians (Gaels) from Iona (Spain) to Ireland, according to the *Book of Invasions*. Since this is the earliest of times, historians have figured it to be around 2000 BC. Amergin does, in fact, have magical powers not at all common with later druids. When he brings the Gaels to Ireland he finds the land is occupied by a deity race known as the Tuatha de Danann. This supernatural race is ruled by an actual god named Dagda (pronounced "Dada"). It is interesting that the Tuatha race has very little difficulty fighting off another supernatural race known as the Formorians, but enormous difficulty fighting the Milesians. The most famed incident to come of the Milesian conquest was when Amergin banishes the Tuatha de Danann to the burial mounds that are scattered in their hundreds across the country. To this very day the burial mounds are believed to be haunted by faerie people.

The great mythological tales of Ireland are kept in four realms of storytelling in Ireland; one of them is called *The Finian Cycle*. It is here we come across our next well-known druid. This is our first female druid, who goes by the name, Bodmall. She shows us that in the druid world there is no sex distinction. I will speak more of this when we talk about the druids of Germany. Female druids had very important roles to play in the Celtic world, though they were very different from those of the male druids. Bodmall is a noted character in the legend around Fionn McCool. The stories are dated to around AD 260. When Fionn is born there is an armed conflict going on within the Tuathe (a county-sized government structure). Fionn's father Gumball is heavily involved in this conflict. The man he is fighting is called Goll MacMorna. In a successful attack on Gumball's fortress Gumball is killed by Goll. Goll wants to kill everyone in the garrison especially Gumball's children, one of whom is the baby Fionn. The druidress, Bodmall comes to the rescue. She takes the child off into the forest away from Goll's soldiers and raises him in her secret dwelling with her sister, Cumhal. Here is also where we come across the wide variety of skills the druids had. In this case, Bodmall and Cumhal are elite fighting warriors. There are hundreds of stories and true historical references to elite fighting women in the Celtic world. From this perspective Bodmal and Cumhal are nothing special. The two women train Fionn to become an elite warrior like themselves. In the end, Fionn's fighting skills are so well developed he ends up being one Ireland's greatest warriors.

A druid whose story I just recently came across was probably Ireland's greatest influence in starting its days as an empire. This is Nair, who served King Eochaid Mugmedon in AD 350. Nair gets overshadowed by the bard, Torna. Torna is well recorded for saving Niall of the Nine Hostage's mother Keran's life from the wicked queen, Mongfind. It's quite a dramatic telling. It is from Torna we learn that Nair spends a lot of time away from Ireland visiting his peers in Britannia. Perhaps it was from Nair that Eochaid picked up an interest in the rest of the world. As it is, Eochaid is noted for having built the greatest naval fleet in the history of Ireland; over 300 ships. We learn more of that fleet when Niall comes to the Tara throne. When it comes to Nair, his continuous traveling at certain times of the year, like during Lughnasah, confirms many of the observations made by Douglas Munro in his book *The 21 Lessens of Merlyn*. Munro states that festivals were very important to the druids. It is suggested that Nair preferred to celebrate them with his peers away from Ireland. Torna, it would seem, was often given the task to sit in Nair's place when he was away. This was a risky move because if the ovate was present, though it sounds like he wasn't either, there would have been a power struggle for sure. One of the big things, which I've already mentioned, is when the druid finished training it was important he was given a job in the kingdom right away. This maintained his status and authority with the Celts. Hiding in a cave somewhere making magic was not a druid characteristic at all.

This next druid was also a real person from sixth-century Breton (France). His name was Gwenc'hlan. Since he resisted becoming Christian, he was imprisoned and then later his eyes were gouged out. How he became famous in his part of the world was that he put a curse on the authorities. This was the first of its kind. It is known as Diovgan Gwenc'hlan (Gwenc'hlan prophesy). Apparently from the sixth century all the way to the nineteenth, whenever anything bad happened it was blamed on the prophesy. The prophesy had such an impact in France that a writer by the name of Hersart de la Villemarque wrote about it in his book *Barzaz Breiz*. It was one of those things the church exploited to illustrate that the druids were indeed mixed up with the devil.

The most renowned druid of all time is, of course, Merlyn in the famous story of King Arthur. In the Welsh legend, Merlyn is given all sorts of magical powers by Geoffrey Monmouth. By the twentieth century, Hollywood has embellished Merlyn's traits so much that we can't possibly imagine anything other than him being all-powerful. Ironically, there was a real Merlyn but he did not live in the same time period as the great King Arthur; he lived a hundred years later up in Northumbria. This Merlyn drew Geoffrey's attention because like Gwenc'hlan, he too was making prophecies and many of them were claimed to have come true. In his time (sixth century) he made quite a name for himself. Since Geoffrey was in the eleventh century he took artistic license and incorporated him into his story of King Arthur. People have to remember that the Merlyn in the Arthur legend is fictional and the real one doesn't come along for another hundred years.

Diviciacus of Aedui is the first full real druid we can make an assessment of. He served Julius Caesar in 55 BC. With Diviciacus an enormous amount of the druid myth is realized. First, Diviciacus is not loyal to Caesar, he is only serving him to protect his people, the Aedui, from Roman wrath. Diviciacus was fully aware of the coming of the Romans into Gaul, so he tried to have his people spared as much of the brutality as possible. He was a brilliant orator and he was allowed to speak to the senate. In doing so, he did manage to win over a number of the senators. As a result, when Caesar marched into Gaul, the Aedui escaped much of the onslaught the rest of the country suffered. This brings up an interesting aspect of the druid world, which is that they were under no pressure to show loyalty to fellow Celts. Their political training was to be loyal to your own master and no other. This revelation gives credibility to the mythological druids such as the ones in the Tain bo'

Cu'ailnge story. The druids serving Maeve of Connaught are not chastised any more than the druids serving Connor MacNessa of Ulster.

Either Caesar didn't understand what Diviciacus was telling him about the druids or Diviciacus was clever enough to always use Roman terms to describe the druid world. From Caesar's Gaul Campaign writings, everything he writes about the druids is in Roman understanding. Diviciacus does not violate the principal rule of druid secrecy. Also, perhaps Caesar was not interested in the cultural side of the druids; only their political authority with the Celts and that was it. As much as we learn about the druid order is as much as we don't learn. It is fascinating that over the years Diviciacus was with Caesar he disclosed very little. Diviciacus turns out to demonstrate the degree of cleverness of the druids as well. Say a lot but tell almost nothing.

Two major points of interest that come from this relationship draw the attention of modern historians and archaeologists—where the major druid centres were. As mentioned before, Diviciacus proves to be a valuable source in this regard. He tells Caesar where the major druid groves are and that the order predates the coming of the Celts. We find from the research done by Francis Pryor that Diviciacus was telling the truth. Diviciacus identified Mona (Anglesey) and Marseille (France). Turns out both are accurate.

Moving on, the next giant of a druid figure takes us into world of bards—the famous Taliesin of Welsh folklore. The reason I say folklore and not that he was a historical figure is because his real existence is still hotly debated. There are as many people who say he is real as there are saying he is fictional. What becomes interesting is all the bards who are credited with his name. There are hundreds of them. If they are fictional, then who wrote them? If they are genuine, then how is it that his existence can't be confirmed?

Taliesin is said to have been born in the fifth century in Northumbria. He later moved to the Powy Kingdom court and made this his home. His greatest bard poem satirized King Maelgwyn of Gwynedd. King Maelgwyn ruled Gwynedd from approximately AD 490-540. The poem was so accurately composed, many historians are convinced from this alone that Taliesin was a real historical figure. Whether he was fictional or not, one thing does come from the writings, which is that he is recognized as a druid. He is the verification that bards were just another stage of the druid training.

In the story of Vercingetorix, who fought against Julius Caesar, we learn of two druids. One is a male and the other is a female. The male druid is Cunicepio. He is involved with the overthrow of a kingdom, which is not an acceptable act for a druid to be taking part in. A druid's role is only to advise and nothing more. Apparently, there is some kind of civil war going on with the Averni Gaul nation, Vercingetorix's father Celitillus is on the losing side, and Cunicepio gets involved in the execution of Celitillus. Years later when Vercingetorix is older he takes his revenge on Cunicepio...which proves why druids were never to get directly involved in politics. When you consider how long it took to train a druid, you can see why it wasn't not in their best interest to get directly involved with the affairs of state.

The other druid(ess) goes by the name of Bria. As in the story of Fionn MacCool, Bria is a druid warrior. In real life, she trained Vercingetorix to become a great warrior. This verifies the story of Bodmall and Cumhall as well the training of Cu Chulainn by Shin Megami Tensi on the Island of Mann.

By this point it should be realized that the relationships some of these druids had with historical figures either ends up verifying their existence or the opposite. The fictional druid testifies to the skills of a real druid and vice versa. Further, it increases the credibility of the mythological stories.

Another druid from this time comes out of the *Book of Invasions*: Iarbone'l. He goes back to the earliest of times in Irish history. He was an arch-druid to a Nemedian king. From a historical perspective, he stands out because he is often used to demonstrate how much of the Celtic culture was adapted from the cultures of the people before them. It is an argument I have already made, and I will be showing more examples of it later. The Nemedians' time-frame is about 1000 BC. If the name is supposed to associate with a real culture, then that would be the Pan Beaker People. Iarbone'l built his reputation on making an abnormally large number of prophesies. Apparently, in the end it caught with him when several of them backfired. This was one of the cardinal rules of the druid order when it came to prophesies and magic—use it sparingly.

The arch-druid to the infamous Queen Mebd (Maeve) was Cailitin Da'na. He was one of the few druids who was badly intimidated by a ruler. Normally it's the other way around. In the legendary story, *The Tan Bo Cu'ailnge*, when Queen Mebd decides she is going to invade Ulster for the Brown Bull of Cooley, she calls upon Cailitin to prophesize how it will turn out. He tells her rather reluctantly it is going to end up in a bloody mess. This is exactly how it does turn out. Though Mebd has the superior numbers, she is frustrated by a single warrior known as Cu Chulainn. He skillfully delays her advance into Ulster when at last the Ulster warriors are able to get over a curse sickness. In the end, Ulster is able to drive back Mebd's forces and at a terrible cost. Cailitin goes down in Irish history as the druid who gave the most profound prophesy of any.

"Bandorai," is a term that originated in medieval times. This is a name given to female druids. The druids, though, just referred to them as druidess; no big mystery here. In medieval times people were fascinated by female druids and so an incredible amount of writing was devoted to the subject. As of the eleventh century, things were learned about them that had not been known previously. Surprisingly, the research was exemplar. Druidesses had a special role in Celtic society. Their main employment was that of being ambassadors, particularly to the Greeks. Greek writers like Strabo, Diocletian, and Alexander Severus spoke often of their visits.

It's not clear if it is sheer imagination or if female druids were trained on the Isle of Man. But this is supported by two writers; Tacitus and Douglas Monroe. If true, the Isle of Man was to the female druid as Anglesey was to the male druid. One particular skill female druids learned was political rhetoric. Even in Roman records it is found that when the Romans wanted to negotiate with certain Celtic nations, they were confronted by a druidess. One druidess specifically named by the historian, Cassius Dio of Rome, is Gonna. He referred to Gonna as a bard. However, when you read up on her you find out she was again the classic druidess ambassador.

Boudicca is a powerful name in British history as the great warrior princess of the Iceni rebellion in 61 AD. There is no dispute she was a real historical figure, who made a huge impact on the Roman Empire. However, recent research has uncovered the fact she actively took part in Celtic religious ceremonies, meaning she was likely a high-ranking ovate. This would account for why a larger than normal number of Britons followed her into battle. Her princess rank alone could not have mustered the manpower she ultimately achieved. Her rebellion, though unsuccessful, is said to have been so impressive she unnerved the Roman emperor Nero himself. He made some sweeping changes to the standard Roman policies of conquest after her revolt. The Romans from this time on had to be more sensitive to the concerns of the Britons. Those policies were best recorded when Agricola came to Briton in 71 AD. He was not so quick to use the sword when it was not necessary.

Another druid was the all-powerful Mug Ruith of Munster. Why he gets special mention is a reflection on the very subject of druid authority. He was a man who had physical presence besides the fact he was a druid, meaning he could likely win a physical fight if it ever came down to it. He is another example of where it is hotly debated if he was historically real. Many claim he was mythical. However, it does seem that for a man who was mythical he was very much involved in the historical event of the expulsion of the Deisi Celts from Munster during the reign of Cormac McAirte (c. AD 261). The Deisi Celts were exiled to Demetae (now Dyfed) due to some unknown disagreement with both the Munster king and McAirte. Mug Ruith is most noted for his unusual longevity. Here's where his mythical qualities come into play. It is said he outlived seventeen kings. If this is true he lived way past one hundred years. Considering the average life expectancy was only forty years, it is a bit of a stretch to make such a claim. However, the time on the throne in those days seldom exceeded twenty years. Also, he is credited for personally training his own daughter Tiachtga to become a druidess. As we know, the common practice was for girls to be sent to the Isle of Man for training; so, Mug Ruith took a chance on getting expelled from the druid order. Here is a verifying point for Douglas Munro's claims that druids were privately trained. They were not sent to a druid school.

Two definitely historical druids a lot of people know about from Irish history are, Lucetmill and Lochris, the arch-druids of King Loaghaire (Leary) in 450 AD. Likely one was an ovate. Their claim to fame is when the druids for the first time went up against a Christian priest...Saint Patrick. They first met in Tara during the Beltane celebrations. The tradition was that before the first big fire was lit, all the fires around had to be extinguished first. Patrick did not abide by the custom and so he was automatically at odds with the king. Patrick challenged the two druids to a contest of magic and as the story goes, Patrick came out on top. This allowed him to spread the Christian religion with the reluctant blessing of the king. After this event, we do not hear of the two druids again. From what is written in the *Annals of Ulster* it's because the two druids disgraced their kind, so they were banned from the kingdom. Again, we are reminded the druids had to be wise about when was the best time use their magic. Two druids in a fit of anger tried to go against a better prepared opponent and lost. This event no doubt had one of the biggest impacts on the entire druid order, for it took a huge amount of their prestige from them. A hundred years later in Ulster at the famed Drumceat Assembly, it came to haunt the druids when King Ainmuire mac Setnai had them completely stripped of all their power. However, it has to be noted that the bards still retained their authority. They were still welcomed by all the courts in the country. This point gets special mention in the tenth century when Brian Boru comes to the Tara throne.

As the sixth century rolled in, the Christians were now coming in greater numbers. One of the big names among the new arrivals was Saint Columcille. He moved from Ireland to Dalriada of the Picts. Then he sailed up Loch Ness to the Pictland capital, Inverness, to meet with the Pictish King Bridei. Like Saint Patrick, he confronted the ovate druid Gradlan in a contest of magic. Again, a Christian saint defeated a druid. The Pictish king was so impressed with Saint Columcille he allowed him to spread Christianity throughout his kingdom. *The Pictish Chronicles,* which were written by monks, claim this was the event that marked the end of druids in Pictland, for Christianity then swept the country. However, the big contradiction to this claim is when Constantine II came to the throne of Scotland c. AD 927. He resurrected an old Celtic custom that he was to be crowned while sitting on the sacred "Scone Stone." In Scotland, the Scone Stone has exactly the same Celtic magic to it as the "Lia Fil" stone of Tara does. A king is not official until he touches the stone. If the Christians had actually completely removed the pagan customs of the Celts from the Picts as it says in their *Chronicles,* then chances are the Scone stone would have disappeared with it. The Scone Stone in Scotland and the Lia Fail stone in Ireland exist to this very day and are important druid symbols to both countries.

The last druid I am going to look at is Veleda. She was a druidess who verifies the importance of female druids in the Celtic world. At the time of Emperor Vespasian, the emperor was trying to resolve a long conflict with the Germans, and so he sent emissaries to negotiate a peace. To the frustration of the Romans, the Germans would only talk with them through their female druid, Veleda. It turned out she was also an ovate; so, once it was discovered the Romans were up to their old treachery, Veleda put a cursed on the Romans. It turned out to be effective. When the Romans sent their legions against the Germans they were ambushed. Due to their victory the Germans celebrated Veleda as a true representative of the gods.

From the people I have mentioned, you likely have, for the first time, an actual glimpse into who the druids were in person. It makes a big difference to know who some of them were, for it certainly removes the mysterious nature of their practices. Druids were not all powerful. They were very human and the key to their success was more about timing than real magic. They did, however, know lots of stuff the average person didn't, so that made them exceptional. The rule of their power was do everything in moderation. As we saw with Lucetmill and Lochris being rash exposed their human frailties. What you are going to see from here on in is how much they knew and thus the reason for their success.

Chapter 5

The Tree Oracle

You have magic in your fingertips,
Magic in your eye.
Magic in the arms that hold
And tell me not to cry.
There is magic in your voice
When you talk to me each day.
There is magic in your smile
And in the things you say.
there is magic in the way
You let me be myself with you.
There is magic that you teach me
To be good and brave and true.
I am growing older
And soon I'll go away,
But the magic that you taught me
Will go with me every day.

Grace V. Tidrow

Trees were of central importance to the druids and is how they got their name; oak teacher/priest. It is amusing that several thousand years later, with the onset of global warming, we are again having the same obsession with trees as the druids did. However, ours is more about survival than it is religious. Mind you, when you see what the druids knew of the functions of the various trees you really wonder if we are that different.

The Tree Oracle or what is more commonly referred to as Ogham, an ancient alphabet, was first discovered by the druids in the first century BC. From a religious standpoint, Ogham is named after the god Ogma, the god of eloquence. It was discovered from the famous story of *Tan Bo Cuailnge.* The famous Cu Chulainn uses this special lettering form to write a message on a piece of wood. This story is dated to the first century AD. It is not until the fifth century when Ogham at last is transferred to stone columns. Ogham originated in Ireland and spread to Britain in the sixth and seventh centuries. From here we at last can decipher the letters and their meaning.

Ogham Alphabet

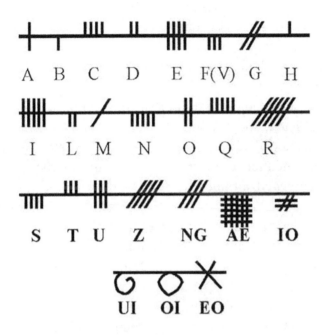

Ogham is a crude, slashing lettering system. It was not only used for written communication, but each letter had a symbolic religious meaning as well. I am drawing heavily on two authors to provide you with the information in this portion of the book. They are: Brendam Cathbad Myers; *the Mystery of Druidry,* and Vanessa Card; *The Celtic Tree Oracle.* There is a single centre line with notches on either side of it. The notches start on the right, then switch to the left and then finally cross over the centre, first horizontally and then on an angle. The notches are in sets of five. Each notch represents a letter, a tree, and a meaning. There is a total of thirty-five letters. I will enclose a diagram of what they looked like. The Ogham system does follow the standard ABC format, but a tree value format. So, what will be quickly noticed is the letters are in a random order. Here you must remember which trees were considered important and which were not. Also, you are going to see that the nature of the tree and its general use by the Celts were involved, thus the reason for its importance based on its function.

What I am going to do in this presentation is show the symbol-letter, the equivalent modern letter it represents, the tree, and finally its meaning. Also the Celtic calendar must be mentioned, for in many cases the special festivals that happened around the year were symbolic to many of the letters. The biggest date that sets everything off is November 1st. This is the start of the Celtic New Year. The festival for this date is called Samhain. The second big date is February 1st. This date marks Imbolc. The third big date marks the second largest festival day: May 1st. This is the day they celebrated Beltane. The fourth significant date is August 1st. On this day they celebrated Lughnasah. This is the harvest day for the Celts. And of course, the year starts again on November 1st. There are two other dates that were important to the Celts and especially to the druids and they were, December 21st and June 21st. The first date marks the Winter Solstice and the second date marks the Summer Solstice.

Beith/ Beth

The first set letter is called **beth** (beh) in Gaelic and birch in English. The letter is "B" which comes off the word beth, not birch. You will notice this later on when you find the Gaelic word is different from the English one. The birch symbolizes a new beginning. It actually has a celebration date; the Samhain Festival of November 1st. The Celtic god it is associated with is Manannan a Mac Lir; the god of the underworld and the god of the sea. The birch, a deciduous hardwood tree, is readily recognized for its predominant colour of white with black slashing marks. There is no serious market for the tree like the soft-wood trees have. The bark is paper-like and the North American Indians used to strip it off for the making of canoes. Also, the bark has been found to have a high concentration of vitamin C, so it is a good source for curing colds and scurvy.

Luis The second letter of the tree alphabet is **luis** (loo-ish) or rowan in English. The letter is "L," which again comes from the first consonant of luis. Rowan represents protection against enchantment and survival. The month you celebrated this symbol was December. There are no Celtic gods associated with this Ogham letter. There are a lot of berries on the rowan, a very large tree, so it attracts a lot of birds. The quality of the wood is such that staffs were made from it. On Beltane it was from the rowan tree that branch arches were made for the cattle to walk through first before being marched between two rows. The idea was that the cattle were being blessed with protection.

Fearn/ Fern **Fern** (fearn) or in English again, the alder. This is the third letter in the Ogham and the letter once more comes from the Gaelic word, therefore it is "F." The alder, a water-loving tree, symbolizes protection against magic. It also provided shelter against the elements. The oily, water-absorbing wood has had an enormous practical use in the foundation of building projects. Since the wood agrees with wetness, it's perfect for construction.

It is said much of Venice is built on rowan logs. The Welsh demi-god Bran is associated with the tree and reinforces the symbolism of protection. The month of December is when this tree is celebrated.

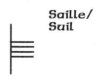

Saille/
Sail

The fourth tree letter is **saille** (shall-yuh). Its letter is thus "S" and the English translation is the willow. This well-recognized water tree is very symbolic of flexibility and protection for good health. The protection goes one step further in that the druids found there was a magical quality to the tree and as a result, all spell wands were only made from these branches. From that, a tradition was started. Willow sticks in general are regarded as protection sticks against evil spirits in the house. There is not a lot of practical use for the wood. When making a blessing with a willow wand it is always done in the name of the god Lugh and Lughnasah is its special celebration date (August 1st).

Níon/
Nín

Next is **nion**, pronounced (nee-on). The letter is thus "N" and the English interpretation is the ash tree. This tree has been designated as one of the five trees of wisdom. From this special appointment, the ash is associated with healing first and foremost. Being a hardwood of good quality, the ash had enormous usefulness for buildinlg in medieval Britain and Ireland. Also, the wood is today the best source for making hurling sticks. In terms of weapons, bows were made from ash.

**Huath/
Uathe** The <u>second</u> set of notches on the stem marker now switch from the right side to the left, starting with a single horizontal slash. This mark begins with the sixth tree being **huath** (hoo-ah) and in English it is known as the hawthorn. The letter is "H." In many cases, because the tree grows so very slowly, it is more often regarded as a bush. These trees are very magical and in the UK and Ireland it is claimed that faeries dance under them. You must show a great deal of respect for the hawthorn. The tree symbolizes magic and guardianship. It was claimed the tree was the doorway to the otherworld. To make any magic work, you had to circle the tree three times. There was a caution with this tree; it was regarded as bad luck to bring a hawthorn into the house.

**Duír/
Daír** Moving right along; the next is the most powerful tree of them all, the great **duir** (doo-ir) or in English, the great oak! The druids treasured this tree above all else believing it had the greatest magic to it. The letter for the tree comes off the Gaelic word so it is "D." One of the things the druids noticed about the tree is that it shed its leaves just at the time of Samhain and started to leaf just at the time of the Beltane festival, and this in itself was special. Sometimes the oak is called the king tree. The great oak symbolizes very good luck. It represents perfect balance. The oak tree is more or less the altar spot for druid practices, that is how sacred it is. As for the wood, it is very hard and durable. Over the centuries it's been used in construction and wood carvings.

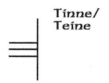

**Tinne/
Teine** The next tree symbol is the **tinne** (chin-yuh) representing the letter "T," and in English it is the holly tree. This is more of a bush than a tree and it is often found on the edge of a forest. It is well recognized for its shiny, pointy, broad leaves and red berries. The holly is one of the great symbols of Christmas. This bush is another symbol for protection but specifically for the house. Thus, when you see it as a decoration out of season, it is for the purpose of home protection. Also, it has been found that when the leaves are boiled the juices can act as a cough medicine. In ancient times, if the wood was long enough, it was used for the centre shaft of a Celtic chariot. There is not much use for the wood today.

Continuing on, the **coll** (koll) with four lashes is next. Again, the letter comes from the Gaelic word, therefore it's "C." In English it's the hazel tree. This tree is covered in nuts come the fall, so it gets a lot of attention from squirrels. Be aware the nuts are good for people as well. They are high in protein, so they help with the liver. The tree symbolizes wisdom and knowledge. There is not much commercial value for the wood. However, druids specifically cut large branches off them to make staffs from them. The wood is resistant to water and wet weather.

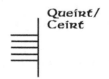

**Queirt/
Ceirt** The **queirt** (kwair-t) or apple tree is the last of this second group. The letter is of course "Q." The apple tree symbolizes beauty and prosperity. They were well aware thousands of years ago that apples are good for you. This was a tree that was protected

by law. It was a serious offence to cut one down. Though it's a tree that provides food, the wood, then and now, has almost no commercial value.

Muín This next symbol starts the third set of five. This group does not have as high an importance as the first set did. The markings are on a diagonal slant and completely cross the stem on both sides. The first one is called **muin** and the letter for it is "M." The English translation is vine. This vine is of course the grape vine, which is not at all common in Ireland but can be found on a limited basis in Briton. However, it's very common in ancient Gaul (France). Seeing that the symbol originated in Ireland, it suggests that it had spread to the continent. It represents sweetness, desire, feasting, and prosperity. In practicality, grapes are not only enjoyable to eat and the primary source for wine, they are also very nutritious. Today wine is one of the biggest products of the food industry and definitely symbolizes a comfortable living if you can afford it as part of your everyday living. The earliest Celts; the Hallstatt Celts in 400 BC, had wine as part of their main diet. However, starting in 250 BC with the La Tène Celts, wine was strictly a drink for the nobles. Everybody else began drinking mead.

Gort The **gort,** which is the letter "G," or in English, the ivy, has a mixed symbolization. Since the berries of some vines are not good to eat, this means that the ivy is not necessary a good thing. The principal meaning to this figure is ambition. However, it also represents healing, since some ivies are actually ideal for medicine purposes. The predominant use of the acceptable ivies is for skin problems. They can be used as ointments. In practical uses the ivy is, for most people, a foliage used to decorate a home. This has been a practice since medieval times.

Moving along in the not-tree representations, the third symbol with three slanted slashes is **ngetal,** pronounced ngyeh-dul. Sure enough, the modern letter for it is "N." In English it means reed. This symbol has several meanings since the reed has several functions in real life. It can be used for medicine. It is used in the roofing of a house and for making baskets. All are positive. Being that reeds are used to attain a specific goal, then its meaning is direction.

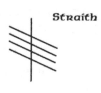

Stʀaíth

Next is the **straith, with the** letter being "S." It represents the blackthorn. The blackthorn is very similar to the hawthorn but has needles where the hawthorn has little stubs. Also, as the description indicates, it has a darker bark to it. Its leading use in medieval times was in making red pigment. It is a very durable colour. Like the hawthorn, this bush is used for fencing by farmers. Apparently in Ireland the wood is particularly strong, so it is very popular for making the famous Irish shillelaghs. This tree shrub has the same magical properties of a hawthorn in that certain trees could very well be faery trees. It calls for strong action that must be obeyed. There is no misunderstanding the message a blackthorn gives.

Ruís The **ruis** represents the letter "R." In English it is the elder. This is the last letter of the slanted, full-cross emblem set. It has kind of a double meaning to it. Depending where you are positioned it could mean the beginning or it could mean the end. Because of its peculiar nature it is definitely connected with the Samhain festival, for Samhain also has two meanings; end of the one year and the beginning of the new-year. In terms of practical functions, the most noted use of the tree is its famous elderberry juice, which is made from the berries. This juice is excellent for colds.

Ailím/ Ailm The **ailm** (al-um), more commonly known as the silver fir tree, is the start of the <u>fourth</u> group of five symbols. The letter is "A." The marking is a straight lateral slash across the main stem. This tree is regarded as one of the "sacred trees" because the sap, when diluted in water, can act as disinfectant for skin rashes or insect bites. Further, the needles can be used in the making of straight tea. In the UK this coniferous tree is harvested as a commercial tree, not only for building but for use as a Christmas tree. It symbolizes peace and long sight.

Onn Next, with two lateral slashes is the **onn** (uhn), the letter being "O," It is the furze in English. This scraggy, bush-like tree is often found in open fields by itself. It gives off a sweet smell and throughout the year always has one or two yellow, tulip-shaped flowers blooming. It is a hardwood and very popular in the making of hurling sticks. This is another tree that is good for making tea from its needles. This tree is more common to Ireland than anywhere else in the British Isles. It symbolizes transformation and is associated with Lughnasah.

Uʀɑ/
Uhʀ

The three-cross slash Ogham symbol represents the **ur** or as some call it, the **ura**. The letter is "U." In English, it is heather. This small bush is most common on mountainsides in Scotland. It does not grow higher than six feet. Though most plants bloom in the spring, its flowers arrive in the fall; so it has its own characteristics. It represents hidden surprises. Its leading commercial value is in the farming of bees, because bees are attracted to the bush at an unusual rate.

E - Eadha

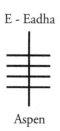

Aspen

Four lateral cross slashes are the **eadha** (eh-ha), the poplar or aspen tree. This tree represents the letter "E." It has a fir-tree-like image from its overall spearhead-like shape. However, it has broad, spearhead-shaped leaves, and so is a hardwood tree all the way. The tree has a unique quality to it in nature. Whenever a forest fire has taken place, the new growth will likely be poplars. This tree symbolizes endurance and strength to persevere.

I, J, Y - Ioho

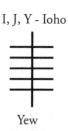

Yew

The last Ogham symbol for this group is the **ioho** (ee-uh):the letter "I," which is the yew tree. This is a broad-leaf, coniferous tree. In medieval times the tree was extremely popular for the making of bows. The wood is strong and flexible. The tree is legendary for being the longest-living tree in Europe. In many cases, the tree can live to be a thousand years old. The tree represents long life, for obvious reasons. However, the Christian church has given it a new meaning; that of death, for the tree is often planted in graveyards. Yews have a menacing, wide base with distorted branches.

This ends the conventional tree Ogham symbols. From here there are five more Ogham symbols but are not trees. They are:

The CH Koad—grove: symbolizing a sacred place.

TH Oir—spindle, representing sweetness and delight

PE Uilleand—honeysuckle; which represents hidden secrets

XI Mor—the sea, which symbolizes travel.

I am of the opinion these have been recently added, for the druids were more into trees than anything else when it came to symbolism.

HOW TO USE THE OGHAM SYMBOLS

There are two main methods to divination when it comes to Ogham symbols.

The first one is the groups of three, which take direction from the Trystan symbol. The Trystan symbol represents past, present, and future. You can have the Ogham symbols on cards or ideally on sticks. If it's cards, make sure you shuffle them well. With the sticks you place them in a small bag and shake it up well.

How it begins is you think of something of importance that has serious meaning to you. The divination is, what is its course? Give it a moment to be fully developed in your mind. The idea is so that the spiritual world can grasp your true feelings on the subject. Once you have done that, if it's cards you draw three, and if sticks; you randomly draw three. The first Ogham symbol represents the past.

The second represents the present and the third represents the future. If the spiritual world has duly identified your thoughts, then the first two cards should be accurate as to the true situation. If not, then the reading is not going to be correct. If yes, then the last card is going to tell you what is going to be the result.

The second method is the circle of five cards or sticks. You draw a circle and divide into quarters. Where the lines intersect in the centre, draw a small circle there. Then number the spaces 1 to 5, starting in the centre circle and then the top space, continuing clockwise. The number 5 should be to your left. The spaces should be big enough to fit the cards or the sticks.

Again, shuffle the cards and think of what you want from a particular issue. This is a progression solution. First card is placed on the fifth space and you go counter-clockwise until you place your last card in the centre. The first card is of course the past and the least value. The fifth card in the centre is the future results. All the other cards tell of the progression this issue is going to make. Again, the first card is crucial. It must tell the truth of what your issue started. If it is not accurate than the divination is not going to be correct.

Lastly, if you have followed the overall principle of the druids' practices, than you will know you do not do this stuff on a regular basis. With Ogham, the rule is you only do it once a month. The second time you use the cards on the same issue, the first card must be representative of it. Druids felt if you couldn't come up with the same card or one close to your subject, then the spirit world was not ready to give additional support.

CHAPTER 6

Druid Medicines

"What's in a name? That which we call a rose
By any other name would smell as sweet."

ROMEO AND JULIET

(SHAKESPEARE)

From the trees we are naturally led into all the different plants, flowers, and herbs that the druids used for medicinal uses. As might be expected, the druids had quite a collection. A lot of it we still use today but are unaware of its origins. On this subject I discovered that many of the medicines the druids had were from foreign areas, particularly the Mediterranean. This leads us to quickly taking a brief look at the world that the druids lived in.

Barry Cunliffe in his book, *Brief History of the Celts*, devoted a whole chapter on the subject of trade that Celts had prior to the arrival of the Romans. Also, a Professor John T. Koche of the University of Wales is currently doing an in-depth study of the general trade traffic that was going on the Irish Sea, again prior to the arrival of the Romans. From these two sources alone, we learn there was an enormous trade going on between the British and Irish Isles and continental Europe. Mediterranean pottery, as just one example, is found practically everywhere, even as far north as Ulster where wine was imported. Archaeologists have found silk clothing in Wales; meaning the trade included Asia as well. According to John Koche, Wales and Ireland were exporting bronze and tin products to the east in return. Roman records show that tin, particularly for the making of mirrors, was highly prized. Tintagel was probably the main trade centre for all the different groups to rendezvous. Right up to the seventh century AD this was a leading trade port.

Knowing there was an enormous amount of shipping going on in the Irish Sea and the English Channel can help explain how the druids were able to get their hands on some pretty exotic medicines. My major source of reference for this part of the book comes from Douglas Monroe's book, *21 Lessons of Merlyn*. He takes much of what the druid pharmacy consisted of from what is claimed to be one of the leading authorities of the druid institution, *The Book of Pheryllt*.

Therefore, from the previous chapter we have the foundation of proof that the druids studied extensively into tree life. So, it should not be so hard to believe they used that same regime in the studying of plant life and its medicinal qualities; or its more notorious aspect; poisons, as was well recorded with Queen Mongfind of Ireland in the fifth century in the *Ulster Annals*.

What I am going to do now is provide a brief list of some of the herbal specimens that were accredited to the druids:

Warning: Do not experiment with any of the following, as it could be unhealthy if you do not know what you are doing.

Lime tree—this bush-like tree looks very similar to a hawthorn. To separate it from being mistaken for a hawthorn, it is nicknamed "the bush." Today the broad-leafed tree is again named the lime tree. The leaves on it are commonly used for making tea. The tea is for a specific use; to treat colds, fevers, and headaches. It kind of acts like an aspirin, in a manner of speaking. It comes as no surprise the fruit is excellent for addressing scurvy. The British Navy used limes quite extensively in the eighteenth century. The tree has its biggest concentration in Britain.

Euphrasia—this weed-like herb is quite small with white flowers. The plant is used for eye infections. The leaves are broken up along with its natural oils, and with a little bit of water it is applied like an ointment. Also, the leaves were used in a tea for the purpose of addressing memory loss. There is no evidence it was ever successful. Lastly, just for a recreational aspect, it was used as a tea as well.

Treacle—grows to about eight inches in total height. Again, it blooms with small white flowers on a stem. It does not look like a very attractive plant. This plant was primarily used for worms. Also, it was used for vomiting, though I am not sure if it was to induce or prevent. The plant has a beautiful aroma, so it was in everyday use as thyme was as a cooking spice. The plant is most abundant in Britain.

Treacle Plant

Bells—sure enough, it got its name from the flower that looks like little white bells. This herb was used for kidney illness. Apparently, in this case, the leaves were cut up to make a soup. It had a bitter taste to it, but recipients knew it was good for them. Also, it was used to address throat inflammation and dysentery.

Tickweed—this slender, single-stem, small, flowery weed grows in a cluster and is a soft, light-purple in colour. The weed is primarily used in external skin use for ailments of a serious nature such as smallpox and tuberculosis. On a less serious note, the weed is used for mosquito and flea bites.

Henbane—looks a lot like a Scottish thistle in terms of its leaves, however, in the spring it blooms a beautiful, large, yellow flower. This appearance could very well be from the fact the flower is Scotland. When it flowers it gives off a lovely scent. I suppose the fragrance is what attracts people and animals to it. The plant actually has a hallucinogenic property and is often included when they make beer. Also, on that note, the weed is semi-poisonous, and if consumed by itself, will cause vomiting.

Lady Slipper Plant

Lady Slipper—this attractive little, wild, single-stem flower is used both as an ointment and an internal medicine. As an ointment its application is for itching and vaginal infection. As a medicine it is used for anxiety and insomnia. Apparently, it has a relaxing quality to it. The beautiful, little slipper flower is not hard to recognize and its colour is purple.

Dittany—is three large, velvety-textured leaves with a small purple flower in the centre. It's definitely a sturdy plant and grows to about thirty centimeters in size. The plant is common to Crete, so, it seems obvious it was shipped to the islands on one of the trade routes. The plant is used for the digestive system and helps with stomach-aches.

Bridewort or meadowsweet—has kind of a prince's lace look to it, with many tiny white flowers coming off one stem. This is certainly a weed. Again, it is another plant that gives off a strong aroma. The plant is used as a pain reliever for general illness like headaches. It's also good for ulcers.

Green Roof Plant

Comicul or green roof, looks a lot like forget-me-nots, being so small and in large clusters. The colour is violet, so that is what distinguishes it from forget-me-nots. It is an edible plant and was often used in the making of salads. For medicinal purposes it is used as a nerve relaxant. Also, if you suffered a spinal injury it was used for that too.

Malva—another big, broad, shiny-leaf plant with a beautiful flower in the centre. This was a plant that was used for throat problems like bronchitis and sore throats.

Arnica montana—the plant looks like a dandelion, but is all yellow. It grows throughout northern Europe and Britain. Its application is as an ointment for cuts and broken skin and also to relieve pain from bruises. It has excellent qualities in healing injuries.

Valeria—this flower-like plant has clusters of tightly grouped, small, violet flowers. The plant can grow up to three feet, so it can grow to be quite high. The root is used as a sedative and mixed in with salad the plant is used to promote sleep. In medieval times it was very popular in northern England.

Saint John's wort—is a small, yellow-flowered, bush like plant, which is very common in southern Europe. If you have been deemed to have bad nerves or to be suffering from back pain, this plant was recommended as an internal medicine.

SPECIAL HERBS:

It is not explained but druids had what was commonly known as faery herbs. It was believed they had magical powers. They were:

- Dandelion
- Eye bright
- Foxgloves
- Yarrow
- Ivy
- Plantain
- Polypody
- Oak

As stated, I am only mentioning a few, for it can be a tedious subject. Yet even from a short list, it is a marvel to realize the extent of what the druids had available for dealing with various illnesses.

On top of this, they were well aware that when someone was sick the person should be kept comfortable in bed. In Ireland they even had recognizable hospitals. From them the druids basically became doctors in treating the ill. Further, it saved them from carrying around their bags of medicine. The first hospitals came into existence in AD 260.

One of the more interesting aspects of druid medical practices was in treating wounds after a battle. Unlike the Romans, the druids were conscious of making sure a sword cut was washed before treating it. They somehow knew that if the wound was not cleaned, it would become infected. Also, they insisted there be no cloth bandages over a small wound if it wasn't necessary. Scabbing was the preferred method of healing a cut. If bandages were required, changing them regularly was another one of their traits. They seemed to be fully aware of the importance of cleanliness when it came to an open wound.

The druids also knew that healthy foods like apples had a powerful effect in the healing process. Next to this, once a person was showing signs of recovery, they knew enough to get the person out of bed and into the fresh air. This was followed by exercise to get the muscles active again.

One of the diseases common in those days was the plague, and the druids were aware that this came on in a high concentration of people, like at Tara. The remedy they found for this was to abandon the establishment. Tara was abandoned on three separate occasions. Since many of the tuathes (tribes) were small, this wasn't a big decision for a small group of people to make.

There was a degree of superstition when it came someone getting sick. When somebody fell ill after doing a great wrong or violating his or her geis, then the druids felt the person was under a spell from the gods. Speaking of which, certain gods like Brigid were called upon to help when a person was sick, for they were the gods associated with health. From this, the druids believed the gods could heal a person as well. This also led to the belief that magical words had the ability to heal, kind of like the stuff that went on with Merlyn. Mind you, one does wonder if it was so much a magical spell versus inducing positive thinking. Doctors today sometimes practice much the same line of thinking where a patient is made to believe they are going to get well soon. In a way this could be construed as modern magic.

Also, another way to help the sick keep their morale up was telling stories by use of a bard and making sure it had a happy ending. They found this was a great way to keep spirits up.

Certain foods were regarded as special and magical in the healing process, like salmon and hazelnuts. Often, a porridge was made to include these two elements. Even without the magic, salmon and hazelnuts are good for you.

Fire was one of the great spiritual elements to the druids and they felt strongly that it had a magical power. Keeping a fire going round the clock was insisted upon whenever a person was sick at home or at a hospital. Again, even without the superstitious element, a fire would keep a patient warm, and if sweating was necessary as in the case of the flu, what better way to deal with it than through a nice warm fire?

Routinely bathing the patient was also insisted upon. This is very interesting when you consider that generally speaking, the hygiene of the Celts was not very good. Yet somehow, the druids knew hygiene was an aspect of helping a person to get over their ailment.

Taking a patient down to a sacred well was also very powerful magic in the healing process. Here it was believed the gods themselves, like Mananann, would directly help the person to get well.

An unusual healing procedure that was implemented was having dogs around. The druids recognized that the comforting nature of a dog definitely helped lift the spirit of an ill person. They made sure dogs were about when someone was ill. Also, it was said that dogs had the uncanny ability to detect if a person was getting worse in their illness or possibly dying. This was the spooky side of the practice.

Certain rituals were practiced when someone was ill. If he/she was at home, the family or friends would walk around the hut three times. The patient, if he was up to it, would be asked to make a circle with his finger three times. And when the person got over his sickness, it was compulsory for him or her to walk around the hut three times as well. Three was a spiritual number. It represented earth, sea, and sky from a religious perspective.

If a person was seriously sick and no one was certain of the outcome, a divination was conducted with the Ogham stones, or a druid would go out and look for an animal oracle divination.

Surgery was practiced by the druids, but it was mostly for the purpose of broken bones. Other ailments treated were skin problems, blindness, cancer, and tuberculosis, which were all addressed through herbs.

This does not begin to fully address the medical practices of the druids, but it does give you a good idea of how they conducted themselves.

CHAPTER 7

The Gods and Myths

Up the airy mountain,
Down the rushy glen,
We daren't go a-hunting
For fear of little men.
Wee folk, good folk,
Trooping all together;
Green jacket, red cap
And white owl's feather!

WILLIAM ALLINGHAM

nderstanding the beliefs of the Pan Beaker and the Urnfield and what they passed on to the Celts is important. Three major practices have now been well recorded, and this gives us an idea of what the tenets of their religion were. The first one is the burial rituals of the two cultures prior to the Celts. They were elaborate and went on for days. The second one was the tradition of throwing valuable items like gold necklaces into pools of water. It is definitely known this custom was passed down to the Celts. The greatest legend to come from it was the legend of King Arthur and his famous sword, Excalibur. The third one was the one the Romans claimed they witnessed on numerous occasions; the ceremonies in the oak tree groves. It is felt the Celtic gods, in particular, were worshipped here. However, what I am going to spend a great deal of time on is the first ritual, because it would appear from the fact the Celts adopted this practice that they felt their strongest protection did not come from their numerous gods, but from their ancestors. The most compelling evidence to prove this point is that Samhain is the most treasured festival on the Celtic calendar.

The origins of the burial rituals seem to have been found by archaeologist Francis Pryor way up in Scotland. He did an enormous amount of research into the religious customs of both the Pan Beaker People and the Urnfield People. The next person who discovered the sequel, so to speak, was again Michael Peter Pearson in his 2005 excavation at Stonehenge. There is a third contributor to this story, and that is William Stukeley. His eighteenth-century research actually gave us the foundation of what we now know of Neolithic religious customs.

Neolithic Age

As stated, where our story begins is way up in northern Scotland on the Orkney Islands at a place known as The Ring of Brodgar. This incredible ring of stones is over 5000 years old. Archaeologists have learned from this place what the stone circles were all about. In the centre of the circle was found the remains of a home. People like Francis Pryor figured it out. What the stone circle represented was an honoring of ancestors. At that very place, probably a thousand years earlier was an actual home and the inhabitants, over time, passed away. Then their descendants raised a great monument in their honour. It is one of the very first examples of what we now realize was the ancient Britons' religious beliefs.

In 2005, Michael Parker Pearson, with a major team of researchers and archaeologists, did what was probably the most intensive dig at Stonehenge, which lasted for almost a year. What was discovered was a confirmation of what was first learned at The Ring of Brodgar; that the place was all about honouring the ancestors. The ancient Britons had an enormous festival at the time of the winter solstice, where they would bring the ashes of their loved ones and either have them buried near Stonehenge or dispersed into the River Avon.

Brodgar Stones

Combining the research of these two sites provided enormous information about the celebrations of the Samhain Festival in Ireland. The Samhain Festival was celebrated on November 1st, very close to the Stonehenge date. Being aware of this opens the doors to knowing how it all worked.

The specific group that archaeologists have now come to recognize as the start of the mixing up of various traditions was the Beaker People. As mentioned earlier, they were the first sophisticated race to come to Britain, circa 3500. It is likely they were the people who put up the first stone circles, which was carried on later by the Urnfield People. The barrows burial mounds are claimed to be another of their great distinguishing practices. Research done by Andrew B. Powell uncovered the fact that many of these early barrows did not face east; which is accepted as one of their defining features. This characteristic did not come into full fruition until 2500 BC, when the Urnfield People arrived.

At this time, a moment must be spent on the differences between a barrow and a passage grave. A barrow is a long, extended, mound grave. The West Kennet long barrow is one of the most renowned examples of this. A normal passage grave is often a huge, round mound like Newgrange in Ireland, which has a long tunnel inside it. Barrows are identified as Beaker People construction and passage tombs as Urnfield.

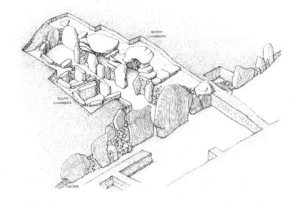

Barrow Burial

What was practiced at a barrow was, in part, passed onto the Urnfield People. At the West Kennet long barrow it was discovered that there was no evidence of human flesh on the bones, meaning the bones were buried after the flesh had either been cleaned off or had been allowed to rot off. Michael Parker Pearson is of the opinion, from what he learned at Stonehenge in 2005, that it was a ceremony of placing a body on a raised wooden platform prior to the body being buried and that the skin was allowed to naturally decay. Once all that was left was the bones, then the remains were haphazardly thrown into a barrow. Thus, it would seem the importance of a person's death was only up until he was physically buried. Each barrow had no more than thirty-five sets of bones in them. In Brittany (France), it was found this number was not consistent. It is claimed that one barrow had the bones of over a hundred bodies, and therefore the 36 body practice was strictly a British custom. Once the barrow had its quota of bones, the tomb was sealed and a new one was built. Evidence suggests that another custom passed onto the Urnfield was that a festival took place prior to the activity of actual burying. There is no evidence that the time of season was important to the Beaker People, which made them distinct from the Urnfield.

From the combined research on the burials of the Beaker People society, some light is shed on what their religious practices may have been. Farming reached Britain for the first time in 3500 BC. This means that the Beaker People went from a hunter-gatherer society to an agrarian one. Now, the weather and seasons played a huge importance in their everyday life. The first references that the sun became a spiritual source come from this era. Miranda Green's research suggests the sun as spiritual source carried on right until the Celts first arrived in Gaul, circa 400 BC. The research done on the Tollund-Man remains in Denmark, has scholars confident he set the standard of how important it was that the "weather/season gods" were appeased. If it was a bad season, chances are that a member of the local authority; i.e. a king, would pay the price. The Tollund-Man was recognized as a man of importance; thus, the theory goes that he was likely sacrificed because there was a bad crop failure. This tells us of the basis for the earliest religious practices.

Bronze Age

Moving onto the Urnfield People, we find things become far more sophisticated and there's a slew of evidence that later becomes associated with the Celts. Again, the Urnfield People arrived in Britain circa 2000 BC, and it would appear they were far more industrious than their predecessors. Most of the stone circles are credited to them. However, it must be noted they were not the originators of these constructions; this is clearly a credit that has to go to the Pan Beaker People. There is, though, an enormous amount of challenge to this observation, notably from Michael Parker Pearson. In his research he finds only partial evidence of Urnfield cultural influence. From what I have learned about the Urnfield to this point and time, who do you believe? What's happening is that a lot of contradictions are surfacing. The centre of it all is Stonehenge itself.

Michael Parker Pearson fully acknowledges that when the burial ceremonies took place they were for the first time centred on the movements of the sun. There were two major festivals that took place at Stonehenge; one on the winter solstice and the second on the summer solstice. Both were huge festivals that went on for days. It started about 1.5 miles up the Avon River at a place called Darrington Walls. Here was another Stonehenge, so to speak, but made entirely of wood. Also, evidence was found of hundreds of temporary houses, thousands of fire pits, and refuse pits filled with half-gnawed animal bones. Clearly this was where the centre of the festival began. It seems the druids wanted to make a spectacular finale to it all and Stonehenge was going to be the highlight.

Pearson surmises that after the feasting, the people gathered up their urns of ashes and started proceeding down the river. Likely many were pouring their ashes into the river as they proceeded. There is a spot south of Wood-henge where six blue stones once stood, and this marks the beginning of a man-made path that turned directly west towards Stonehenge itself. No doubt the druids timed it perfectly so that when the people crested the hill they would see the sun perfectly positioned in the centre between two of the great "Trililthon" stones. It would have been a moment of tremendous awe! From here they proceeded to the stone circle and conducted some form of religious ritual. Afterwards, they went up to the great "Cursus," which was a one-mile-long, dugout mound and on the east side stood a single megalith. Maybe another ceremony was conducted here and finally everybody would go back to the Wood-henge.

The burial ceremonial was an event that revealed an interesting phenomenon. It was not just a local event. Archaeologists realized the solstice ceremony involved the people from all over the British Islands. As mentioned before, it was at Wood-henge that researchers found thousands of pieces of clay pottery and from their unique designs surmised that they had originated from all across Britain, including Scotland and some even from Ireland.

Also, from this time period and on, new circular burial mounds start to appear as well and an exceptional number of stone circle grows exponentially. There is a distinct change in the cultural practices.

Scholars assert that the people of this time had fully distinguished there are four seasons with each very important to note, and this is when new gods start to appear.

Religious ceremony is now a very real part of everyday life. No doubt it is at this point the druids started to command serious authority over the community. We know it was the druids on account of two things that are fully recognized as part of their cosmos practices; the 18.9-year solar calendar and the thirteen-day lunar cycle. Both have been confirmed to Stonehenge and Carrowmore, Ireland. I am going to started sounding like a broken record at this point because this is another practice that was specifically passed down to the Celts. The important thing here is to realize that certain religious practices recognized as Celtic were in fact originated from the two previous civilizations.

Next is the monumental subject of the easterly direction of all the stone circles as well as the burial mounds. As most know, the two places that have the biggest reputation for this phenomenon are Stonehenge and Newgrange, Ireland. Both are dated to 2500 BC. Again, it is a significant time period in Neolithic history. The easterly direction of the openings is exact. The measurements come on the summer solstice of Jun 21st and winter solstice of December 21st. What is most interesting about this subject is it is fully recognized as a druid custom and dated to 2500 BC. There is no question on this point and so it goes without question the druids are dated to 2500 BC. It is one of the strongest arguments as to when the druids came about.

From all of this we have a pretty good idea of what the religious deities were. Elements of the natural world, particularly the sun and the moon, were their gods. However, it was verified from Stonehenge and Newgrange that for personal protection you worshipped your ancestors. The building blocks for the all the succeeding races like the Celts were now laid down.

The Iron Age

We come at last to the arrival of the Celts in 400 BC. There were two major migrations with distinct cultural identities. As such the two groups have been awarded different names. The first migration from 350 BC, which mostly moved into Western Europe, were the Halstatt Celts. In 250

BC, the second migration occurred with another group; the La Tène Celts. They penetrated as far west as France and England but no farther. Moving east was their biggest effort. They swept into Greece, Romania, and modern-day Turkey. This second wave adopted just as many practices from the now-three predecessors; so, in fact, they are no different than the Halstatt.

The big separation between the Beakers/Urnfield civilizations and the Celts is that the latter had an enormous deity pantheon. They had literally thousands of gods. There were certain basic ones that unified the whole people right across Europe. An example is the god, Lugh. He may have had a different name on the continent compared to the British Isles, however, he was recognizable as the same entity; the god of many skills. I am going to quickly break down the fundamental gods and show that the core mentality behind them was exactly the same as it was with the Neolithic beliefs, meaning they had adopted beliefs of their predecessors. What it shows is how the druids became entwined with the Celts and passed down their religious practices to them. What this says is that much of what we today understand to be Celtic was in fact Bronze Age.

The Continental Celtic Deity.

One of the first continental Celtic gods was **Visusicus**. Apparently, he was a fairly widely known god in eastern Gaul and western Germany. Julius Caesar couldn't remember his name, so he wrote him up as the Celtic version of the Roman god, Mercury. Visusicus was a god who controlled the passage to the other world. He is comparable to the British god Mananann, in this regard. In appearance he has horns so he is often mistaken for the god Cernonus, who does not have horns but deer antlers. This god's traits are mostly in divination; so, he was special to the druids. Other traits were that he was a good luck symbol for travelers, and he was the god of poetry and elegance. In Ireland these traits are associated with the god, Brigid. Finally, Visusicus is believed to have originated from the Etruscans.

The next Celtic god primarily honoured in Gaul was **Lenus**. He was recognized as a healing god, similar to Brigid in Ireland. However, Caesar got him mixed up and referred to him as the Celtic version of Mars. Mars was the god of war in Rome. Maybe where the Romans got confused was that Lenus was the god of healing, particularly in battle. He was also recognized in southern Briton by the Cantii and Icenii tribes. In Germany he was fairly common with the Tueton tribes. He was the earliest Celtic god associated with healing fountains and wells.

The god **Suleviae** was definitely a La Tène god, who was widely known throughout the whole of Europe except Ireland and Scotland. He even reached Galacia (Turkey). This god was the god of good leadership. To the Celts, good leadership was extremely important. They elected their kings and so as long as their king wanted to stay in power, he/she had to govern wisely.

On the continent this goddess was known as **Epona**. Her equivalent in Briton was **Rhionon**. She was first and foremost the goddess of the horse. However, she was also noted as the goddess of fertility. Since horses made up much of the Celtic culture, this goddess got a lot of attention. Celts were well recognized for their powerful chariots. Being a skilled horseman was an essential skill of the Celts.

Carvings of this goddess were fairly common throughout Europe, which reflected her popularity.

Cernunnos was one of the most recognized gods of the Celts. His image is immortalized on the famous Gundestrup Cauldron in the National Museum of Copenhagen. He is the god with antlers, and later the church demonized him as the devil himself. He was highly praised for being the god of the animals. The Celts had an enormous respect for wildlife and they were well aware of the importance of conservation—only hunt what you need and no more. In their time they saw certain animals like the red deer and the Britain bear go extinct due to over-hunting practices. This was largely due to the callous attitude of the Romans.

Another powerful name in the Celtic religion is one known as **Lugus** in Gaul, **Llieu** in Briton, and **Lugh** in Ireland. When Caesar was first trying to figure out the various Celtic gods, he got him mixed up with Visiusicus. Lugus is special to the Celts principally because he is the god of the harvest. There is a feast that is celebrated in his honour; Lughnasah, which is celebrated on August 1st. He is one of the first gods for which there is a family lineage. He is the son of the gods Cian and Ethniu. In Ireland, a famous legend tells of when he was confronted by a guard from Tara on what skills he had, and he replied that he had skills in hundreds of arts. He is recognized as the god with the fiery spear that cannot be stopped by any shield.

One of the few Halstatt gods is **Alaunus**. This god had a widespread following in Gaul and in southern Britain in Cantii territory. He was recognized for healing and prophesy, a trait that was very similar to that of Brigid and particularly Ogma in Ireland. You will see that over the centuries certain subjects like healing had overlapping gods. This was one of them.

One of the more notable Gaulish gods was **Alborix**. The meaning of the name is, "King of the Land." It is claimed that it was the source of the name "Albion," which often refers to Scotland. Caesar wrote of this god but addressed him as the Celtic version of the Roman god Mars. He said Alborix matched the Roman god perfectly in all his traits. However, this is not quite accurate. Mars protected the Roman legions, but Alborix protected no one. Like Morrigan of Ireland, Alborix simply sat back and observed a battle. In some cases he gave a sign through a raven about who was likely to be winning it. I will mention this again when I come to the Irish god Morrigan, who sent a crow as her sign of who was to win a given battle.

One god that survived into today's world is the Gaulish god, **Ankou**. He is the god of death. Across France numerous surviving Roman-built fountains have carvings of this god. It's not clear at all why an image of Ankou would be carved into a fountain. This god is very comparable to the Irish Banshee, who comes to collect the soul of the dead and protect the grave. In medieval times this god took on a more sinister image as being one of the horseman of death. He is the horseman carrying the scythe. This god is pure Celt; there is no association with the Urnfield People at all.

Anvallus was a very high-ranking Gaulish god claimed to be only second to Dagda himself. His name is inscribed on numerous Roman Gaul altars; so, it implies there was some degree of tolerance of druid practices allowed, though overall druids were outlawed by the Romans. August is the month dedicated to this god, so, the god can be associated with the Irish god Lugh. They both have similar ranks in their deities.

There are hundreds more Gaulish gods that could be mentioned but I will end it with **Veraudunus**. He was the sun god and very popular up in the north-east end of Gaul, particularly with the Belgae tribes. According to Amanda Green, this god was symbolized with what looks like a wagon wheel on a stone carving. What it actually represents is the sun in a very crude manner. It is believed Veraudunus is represented on the Gundestrup Cauldron. This god is very high ranking among the Celtic Gaul deities but it is not known exactly where.

What I have shown here is a very small sample of the Celtic gods from the mainland of Europe. Many of their legends were eradicated with the coming of the Romans. How some survived was when Gaul became Roman. As one example, it was permitted to inscribe their names in Roman architecture. But there are few myths about them as is the case in Ireland and Wales, and very little is known about them. Still, what is good is they did manage to survive, and we know today about who could be described as the universal gods in Celtic society. A case in point is that names like Dagda, Cernuous, and Lugh are examples of that. Not only were they known in the British Isles but also on the mainland too. It is one more element of the unifying identity with all Celts. I started with the mainland for it is generally accepted the Celts originated in Austria and migrated west. Once mixed in with the local existing Urnfield People they started to adopt their spiritual practices into their own.

Irish Celtic Gods

Logically, I should be proceeding with the Briton Celtic gods next. However, the Celtic Britons were Brethonic Celts and as we know, they evolved as a society well after the Halstatt Celts. This means the next country's gods to look at are the Irish, for they were Halstatt Celts. What is great about the Irish Celts, is that since they were never conquered by the Romans, their religion survived the longest, and so we have probably the best examples from the Irish of any former Celtic nation.

From the Irish we have our best glimpse of the hierarchy of gods and a clear understanding of another group of beings known as demigods. Demigods constitute a person with supernatural powers, who is human in the flesh.

Next, we also have the history of the gods and their demigods; something we never know from the continental gods.

Lastly, it is from their highly developed system we learn of their major festivals and who are the mediators for their gods. What I thought I would do is first show the structure of the Irish gods, then a little of their system, and finally how it all goes together in their religious practices.

Irish Gods

The *Book of Invasion* is where all information on the Irish Celtic gods originated from. This book tells of how five major mythological invasions happened in Ireland. The last and the most significant group of invaders is known as the Tuatha de Danann. This means the "Tribe of Danu" in Gaelic. This is the group where most, if not all, their gods come from. These gods can and did mix with mortals and from the exchange created the demigods. It is not much different from the Greek mythological system. For example the Greeks had Hercules and similarly the Irish had Cu Chulainn; both were men of extraordinary power and ability.

Dagda, pronounced "Da-da" is the supreme god of the Tuatha order. He is described as a large, hooded man and depending who is telling the story, either carries a staff or a massive club. He is compared to Odin in the Viking system and Zeus in the Greek system. That should give you a relative idea of who the man is. From him all the other gods emerge. Admittedly, since he is the top god there is a strange paradox in that other gods come onto the scene, especially female gods and we have no idea where they came from. All we know is that they existed and ended up mating with Dagda to create even more gods. This, by-the-way, we find is one of the signature characteristics of Dagda. He has a ferocious sexual appetite. He is forever bedding every female goddess he comes across. I think when you look into the sexual behaviour of the Celts in general, you may now know its source. Their top god was all about sexual prowess, and so that example was passed down to the people in general.

Cian is a highly ranked god next to Dagda, but his origins are from the Fomorians. The Formorians predate the Tuatha De Danann. Since there is no proper time-line for Cian, it is not clear if he is equal to Dagda in terms of power. How this god became so important is that he and his wife, Ethinui, gave birth to one of the most recognizable names among the Irish Celtic gods; Lugh.

Lugh, pronounced "Lu," is, you might say, the Thunder God of the Celtic Deity. He has a fiery spear that never misses its target when he throws it. Many associate him with the Viking god, Thor. He is a warrior god and does get himself into a lot of scrapes. He is often called "Lewy the Long Arm." Principally, he is a warrior god from one of the tales in the *Ulster Cycle*. From that Cycle we learn Lugh is the god of all talents. The Lughnasagh harvest festival on August 1st is dedicated to him. His most noted act was fathering the great Cu Chulainn from a mortal woman, giving birth to the first demigod.

From here there is a flurry of other gods, all very important, but of course they do not have the same type of power as the ones mentioned.

Lir, pronounced "Ler." He is the supreme god of the seas, but oddly enough there is not much known about him. There is only one story about him in the *Ulster Cycle* and that is called the "Children of Lir." Lir becomes an important deity when he sires Manannan Mac Lir.

Manannan Mac Lir oddly enough, becomes more powerful than his father. Not only does he take over being the supreme god of the sea, but he is the guardian of the underworld. You must get his approval to be allowed into Tir na nOg. Tir na nOg is the otherworld that Celts believed they went to when they died. It is often referred to as the Land of Eternal Youth. The festival of Samhain is partially dedicated to Mananann, because all the spirits can only come to this world by way of him. The Isle of Man, which sits between Britain and Ireland is named after him.

Brigid is one of the top female gods in the Celtic world. She, like Danu, is recognized in most of the islands and on the continent. She has a festival on February 1st known as Embolc. Brigid holds a high rank in the deity on account of the fact she is the daughter of Dagda. She represents healing, fertility, and poetry. There is still quite a debate on whether the sixth century saint, Brigid was an offshoot of Brigid.

Ogma is the god of writing and poetry. It is from this god the famed Ogham comes. The lettering is a series of controlled slash marks. Each slash represents a tree and has a very spirit meaning. Much of the druids' divinations come from Ogham.

Morigan, depending on what cycle you read, has different roles, but all are associated with death on the battlefield. As a result, some refer to her as the goddess of death. Some compare her to the Viking goddess of Valhalla, since she is always seen when a war is about to take place. There is a well-known story in the *Ulster Cycle* where she tries unsuccessfully to seduce Cu Chulainn.

Macha is a goddess primarily from Ulster and is often spoken of in the *Ulster Cycle*. She has many of the same traits as Brigid, where she is again representing fertility and healing, especially after birth. Also, she is associated with horses and has similar powers to the continental goddess, Epona. Macha's special power is her ability to outrun a horse.

There are, of course, dozens more gods and goddess in the Irish mythology, but these ones are the most noted. From here I am just going to briefly mention a few of the most recognized demigods and then move onto the festivals.

Demigods

There are three significant demigods in the Irish mythology. One is a transplant from Wales that I will mention again when I start to address the Welsh deity system.

The first one is none other than the famous Cu Chulainn. He was a powerful warrior that came out of the *Ulster Cycle* in the tenth century. As mentioned, his father was the god Lugh and his mortal mother was Deichtine, sister to the king of Ulster, McNessa. Cu Chulainn means "the Hound of Cullen." His original name was Setanta. How he got the famous name was he accidentally killed the guard dog of a local farmer, and he swore he would guard the farm until the farmer could replace the one he'd killed. Cu Chulainn was noted for going into a disfiguring rage when in battle. Once he was in his zombie-like state, there was no one who could beat him in a fight. Also, he had a magical spear called the "Gae Bolg." When he threw the spear, like Lugh's spear, it always hit its intended target with dreadful results. There is a great story called the "Tan Bo Cuilnege" (Tan bo Cooley). This is the legend of a Queen Maeve of Connaught invading Ulster in pursuit of a valuable bull. In it, Cu Chulainn inflicts terrible casualties on Maeve's army and in the end, despite all the loss of life, she loses the bull anyway.

The second great demigod in Irish mythology is the great Fionn MacCumhail (Finn MacCool). He was a super hero too, of incredible strengths and abilities. His story begins when he is told as a boy to help with the cooking of a magic salmon by a druid. He burns his finger and instinctively sucks it to relieve the pain. And in doing so, he takes in the magic juices of the fish and acquires its special wisdom. From here, Fionn grows up to be a great warrior and starts the famed Fianna elite warrior band. Historical evidence appears to support the fact this was a real entity in Ireland's past. What is known from the *Fenian Cycles* are dozens of stories told of the man and his great feats. He is dated to the third century in Ireland.

The third great mythological legend originated out of Wales in the second century. This is the story of Bran. He is sourced from the Mabinogonion legends. However, since his main story centres in Ireland, the Irish have taken him as their own. The story is that the king of Ireland came over to marry Bran's sister. Things go terribly wrong at the wedding and this affects the marriage when the couple goes back to Ireland. Bran's sister sends a message via a carrier pigeon that she is being mistreated, so, Bran goes off to avenge her. This results in a brutal fight where Bran becomes mortally wounded. His dying wish is to have his head cut off and buried in Londinium, facing south. Today it is said that where London Tower now sits is where the head is buried. The legend goes that as long as the head faces south, Britain will never be invaded.

Welsh Gods and Demigods

It will be found that much of the Welsh mythology is similar to the Irish. But it has been found that the Welsh had more of a matriarchal system than anywhere else. Another thing is the Welsh have the same festival calendar as the Irish; for example, Beltane and Samhain are two of the most important dates in their calendar as with the Irish. Once again, there are numerous Celtic gods in the Welsh system. I am only going to cover a limited number of the more important ones. In some cases, it will be found that with only a slight alteration in the name, the same god/goddess is in the Irish hierarchy.

The Great Don, is probably the highest-ranking goddess in the entire Welsh pagan deity system. Interesting that the top person is a female instead of a male. She is easily endowed with the same power and authority as Danu of the Tuatha setup. She is often referred to as the Goddess of Light, possibly meaning she is the equivalent of the Sun God. All other gods and goddesses answer to the Don.

Arawn, god of the otherworld. To a certain extent, Arawn has many of the same traits as Mananann, when it comes to being the custodian of the afterlife. However, there is one exception to Arawn, he comes out on Samhain and flies about with the living. He returns to the otherworld once the night is done.

Bran (the Blessed) has already been mentioned in the Irish system. Once his head was buried in Londinium, he took on supernatural powers that elevated him from being a demigod to the full status of god. His power is the protection of Britain in the event of invasion or attack.

Hafgan is a bit confusing to figure out. He was once subservient to Arawn but grew in stature to where he achieved authority not only over the underworld, but to a large extent, the living world. It is not fully explained what specific powers he had, though in any case, they did not equal those of the Don.

Mabon is the young god. I suppose he is the protector of youth, from what is said about him. The nickname they have for him is "The Divine Child." The image they have of him is of a boy riding a horse being accompanied by a dog. He is celebrated on the Autumnal Equinox.

Manawydon is the son of the Irish god, Lir, thus proof-positive there is an interchange of religions with the Irish and Welsh. He is exactly the Welsh version of Mananann. As such, they too believe that the Isle of Man is named after him.

Aeronwen is the equivalent of the Irish Morrigan. She is the goddess of war. Unlike her Irish counterpart, Aeronwen determines the winning side, by means of the raven passing over a battlefield. This, by-the-way, was also a practice on the main continent. If I have it right, if the raven flies towards you it means you will win the fight. The opposite direction means you will lose. Like Morrigan, Aeronwen's colour is the colour black and her image is that of the raven.

Arianrhad is a very popular goddess amongst the Welsh people, for she is the protector of women. She is the goddess of the moon and the daughter of the great goddess, Don. She has a lot of authority and is well respected.

Blodeuwedd is the goddess of the night. Her character image is that of the owl. She protects all women who are to be put into forced marriages. Being the goddess of the night is not a blessing but a curse.

Bradwen is the sister of Bran and like him originally a demigod. However, once she dies she becomes a god like her brother. Her story is she was in an abusive relationship with the king of Ireland. From this, she became the goddess to protect women in abusive relationships. From her we learn that the Welsh were far more sensitive to the needs of women than anywhere else in the British Isles.

Cerridwen is a goddess who is still popular today amongst the modern-day witches of Wicca. She is a herbalist, a shapeshifter, and a protector of cauldron magic. You look to her when you want a cauldron spell to be effective.

When you see in a movie or read in a book of a witches trying to conjure up a spell, the concept comes from the Welsh.

Rhiannon is another very popular goddess. She is the goddess of poetry and song, much the same as Brigid. She is also the horse goddess, much the same as Epona and Macha. Being of poetry and song she also represents love. With so many endearing traits it is small wonder why she was so popular.

Govannon will be my last god for the Welsh. He is the protector and representative of the smiths and jewelry artisans. Again, he has many traits that can be compared to those of Brigid.

As can be seen, the Welsh gods and goddesses have many traits that can be compared to the Irish. It proves there was an interchange between the two peoples, even though the Irish were Goidelic Celts and the Welsh were Brethonic Celts. There is an obviously higher presence of female goddesses in Wales than anywhere else. From looking at the extensive number of female gods, it would appear Marion Zimmer Bradley had some validity in her novel *The Mists of Avalon* with its numerous female druids . Even Douglas Monroe's book *21 Lessons of Merlyn* claims that a high number of druidesses in Wales is authentic.

CHAPTER 8

The Magic of Astronomy

I heard them as I rode the Martian tide of sand;
I heard them in the empty air,
I heard them as the reaper stalked outside,
Behind a membrane woven from a prayer,
They spoke to me beyond my earthly sense,
They filled my mind;
they whispered without tongues,
If there's no food, they said,
you should dispense with hunger,
and what use have you for lungs?
Come sail with us through rosy Martian skies,
Unfettered by your useless, choking skin...
And as I fled the famine of my eyes,
A vast and savage bliss unfurled within.

NINA PARMENTER

T he studying of stars was not exclusive to the druids. It is found that the Greeks, the Egyptians, and the Mesopotamians were all examining the stars and planets at the same time as the druids were. The only differences are that the druids' knowledge was seen as magical due to the fact they were living with a people who were far more superstitious than the Mediterranean people. As a consequence, the things they revealed had a much bigger impact.

The druids however, did make advancements on this subject that exceeded their more sophisticated Mediterranean counterparts. The first one was their 18.5-year celestial calendar. It must have taken an amazing amount of patience to have figured that out. The next one is their thirteen-year moon orbit calculations. From examining the sun and the moon, they realized that a complete cycle for the sun takes 18.5 years and for the moon's cycle it takes thirteen years. It was Michael Parker Pearson who was one of the first to figure this out at Stonehenge, though it was first mentioned but not examined in the eighteenth century. People like William Stukeley knew of it but never pursued it to learn how the druids had figure it out. How it was determined in modern times was through the fact that the earth does not have a straight, or a smooth elliptical orbit. Due to its polar gravitational pull, the planet is on a bit of a wavy contour circuit. It bounces in and out of the main orbit. The disruption has effects on the moon and the earth's orbit around the sun. The druids figured out that the complete cycle of the distortion takes thirteen years for the moon and 18.5 years for the sun (which in fact is the earth and not the sun). The way Stonehenge was built, the sun and the moon can be best examined there. It is known the same phenomenon also holds true for the smaller stone circles, however, since most of the stone circles are missing a lot of their original stones, it is much harder to determine how they operated in the same fashion.

Next is the rising of the sun in the east and the setting in the west. This was a huge subject with the druids. There are over 3000 stone circles across Western Europe and just about all of them are set up so that the opening to them is in the east. Most notably, like at Stonehenge, the easterly opening is lined up on the summer solstice. And it is also precisely lined up on the west side for the winter solstice. This same phenomenon holds true for some 1500 passage graves as well. Except for in northwest Ireland, all the passage graves line up their opening to the summer solstice in the east only, not the winter solstice. Another interesting little point is that the lining up is precise to where ever you are in Europe. This point was discovered in Scotland. The easterly alignments are not the same as they are in southern England. Scholars have figured out the druids were aware the sun rises and sets on a more southerly side of the horizontal line in Scotland, and so they lined up their stones to address this uniqueness. It shows you just how perceptive the druids were when it came to the sun and moon's activity.

Now here is a variety of different aspects of astronomy that we take for granted today, but two thousand years ago it was a very magical piece of knowledge to have. When you combine it with some of the specifics that I mentioned earlier, then of course it adds a great deal to the perception that it was magic.

As stated, the druids knew as much about astronomy as did the Mesopotamians did. They were aware of four planets that circled the sky at certain times of year; Venus, Mars, Jupiter, and Saturn. Being seen most frequently in the sky, Mars and Venus got the most attention. Mars' orbit is such that it takes over 687 days to circle the sun and so it is seen on a biannual basis. When it does appear to the naked eye, it is more commonly seen in the eastern sky in the early hours of morning. Venus, having its own orbit, would be seen off in the northeast sky at night and moving on an independent track compared to the rest of the stars. Since the Greeks knew that Mars and Mercury had elliptical orbits, it's not unfair to say the druids were aware of this too. The Greek writers talked a lot about the exchanges the druids had with the Greek scholars, so the sharing of knowledge must have been extensive.

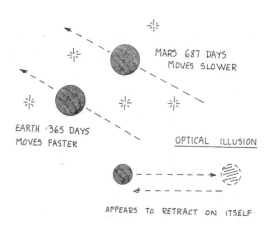

Earth and Mars Orbit

The elliptical pattern is caused by the fact that Earth's orbit moves faster than that of Mercury and Mars. At a certain point, as Earth is perfectly lined up with Mars, its inside track moves faster than the other planets, who appear to be falling behind and look as if they are moving backwards. Once Earth is farther along its path as it starts to disappear on the other side of the sun, the other planets again are seen moving forward. Since the druids were not aware that the Earth circles the sun, all they saw was a bizarre forward and backward movement of the two planets.

How the druids knew that Venus, Mars, and the others were different was by simply following the pattern of all the other stars. It is easy for us today to notice that the Big Dipper not only is the closest to the North Star, it also points to it. The druids would have noticed it as the easiest reference point to use in realizing the North Star does not move. It stays fixed in one location and all the other stars rotate around it. When you realize all the stars are going around in a circle; seeing Venus crossing that pattern naturally stood out. Depending upon the season, with Venus being the brightest star, it will either be high in the northeast sky or near the horizon line. Clearly it does not follow the pattern of all the other stars.

Because there was no pollution as there is today, the druids were able to see a lot more stars than we can. From that perspective, astronomers claim that the druids would have even been able to see the Milky Way in August. They would have witnessed on an annual basis the shower of shooting stars, which even today is a common occurrence in that month. In terms of prophecy, you know the druids could use that piece of knowledge quite effectively against someone they didn't like, perhaps by claiming their enemy was disliked by the gods and the evidence was the shower of meteorites.

Coming back to the movements of the planets, an interesting point was revealed in the fourth century by a bard named Torna. Via oral tradition, he was perhaps the first to discover the back and forth movement of Mars and Jupiter. Seeing a planet move back and forth across the sky must have been a real scare to everyone. Again, it was an optical illusion caused by the short orbital path of earth and the longer paths of Mars and Jupiter. However, 1,600 years ago they did not know this. As such when the strange pattern was formally noted to the primitive culture it would have been regarded as an act of the gods. It wasn't until the 15th century that this phenomenon was scientifically realized.

The moon was the primary source to measuring of time. The druids knew the moon appeared twelve times a year and they measured all their days off it. As mentioned earlier, they even knew the moon had a specific pattern cycle that completed itself precisely in 13 years. Also, they knew there were approximately 365 days to a year and that about two-thirds of that time you could grow grain and graze farm animals. Roughly, they knew there were four seasons and they created a calendar around it. Each season was marked with a festival, like Samhain, Beltane, Imbolc, and Lughnasah. These festivals helped remind the people of certain activities they should be conducting at certain times of the year. The druids realized that by keeping to the festivals the people made the best use of the seasons when it came to their food supply.

By this point it should come as no surprise they were closely examining the behaviour of the sun and the moon in each of the four seasons. In the summer season, both the sun and the moon sat high in the northern sky. In the winter, they sat much lower and neither the sun or the moon would stay in the sky for very long, meaning the days were shorter in the winter. What is the most spectacular part of it all is how they realized when the shortest and longest days were. It becomes an amazing feat when you consider they did not have anything that told them how many hours there were in a day. Today we know that when the earth meets these points in the season, the length of the day stays the same for three days. The blue stones at Stonehenge verify this observation. There are four stones in a rectangular pattern that sit right behind the blue stones and accurately mark out the seasonal changes.

Another anomaly they would have noticed since they were watching the sky each night so carefully, would be the annual Aurora Borealis. In northern Ireland and England this phenomenon was regularly seen in February between the times of 9:00 pm to 1:00 am. No doubt the druids would have tried to make something special of this as well.

Comets were a special phenomenon. They were not seen very frequently but were always perceived as a bad omen. Hailey's Comet is the most noted comet of them all. It has an orbit that it completes every seventy-four years. Basically, the druids would have witnessed this phenomenon once in every century. With their strict oral-tradition standards, there is no doubt they had a rough idea when to expect it next. This would have been the most highly regarded event of all.

Next, we have the solar eclipse. This was another startling event the druids would have made into a bad omen as well, considering the moon blocked out the sunlight. We know today that solar eclipses happen at least three times a year. Unfortunately, they don't happen in the same location each time. In the northern hemisphere, seeing a solar eclipse (total and partial) may happen every five to seven years. That's close enough and regular enough that the druids would have figured out some kind of pattern to them. The other phenomenon is the lunar eclipse, where the earth is between the moon and the sun. It's interesting to note which of the Celtic kings were recorded as seeing both kinds of eclipses as bad omens. Now there has not been a thorough examination of this yet, but they do know from certain generalities in such books as *The Book of the Four Masters* that certain kings were cursed by a sign by the gods in the heavens. One such king said to be cursed was King Cormac MacAirte (c. 260 AD). It was at this time a lunar eclipse had happened. In his case they prophesized his reign was plagued by a bad omen. Unfortunately for the druids they goofed this time. Cormac MacAirte's reign was one of the prosperous in Irish history. This line of thinking was found again during medieval period, notably with William the Conqueror. At the time he invaded England in 1066, a comet was spotted, and it was said the Saxons were cursed by its appearance. So, it goes to show that when strange celestial events occurred, the shamans or even priests claimed it was a sign from the gods.

What we today take for granted 2000 years ago was fully recognised as mysterious magic. We have standard measuring devices at our disposal to accurately tell us when the next celestial event, like a lunar eclipse, is to take place. Such devices did not exist in the Iron Age. So, for a person to come up and say they could predict the next solar eclipse was a fantastic marvel. But when you see how the druids did it, it wasn't magical at all. Each night they would sit out in a field and just watch the skies. They would see the stars rotate, they would see the Milky Way, they would see shooting stars, they would witness comets, and they would see lunar eclipses. Over a long period of study, they would be able to see a pattern in the star behaviour, and after a century or so of passing down their knowledge through their oral tradition, they were eventually able to make predictions.

CHAPTER 9

The Druid Animal Oracle

Where wild horses thunder she can be found
Bestowing to our kings the royal ground,
Their oath as solemn as any marriage vow
In ancient rites by which they are still bound.
If flowing equine manes seen in a glance
She is there by more than mere circumstance
Epona, goddess of fertility
Can we feel her blessings or be mumchance?
Yet also seen as a nymph of warming springs
The gentle caress where e'er nature sings
Like the wild horses there's no holding her
But we can still see what her message brings
I pray I find the need deep within me,
Her desire to be running wild and free

JEMMY FARMER

By now you should realize that everything was sacred to the druids. Not only were the trees sacred but from such gods like Curnonus and Epona, so was the animal life. Like the Tree Oracle every animal had its own symbol. The ovates were the druids who defined the meaning of a certain animal sighting. From it they would determine your divination. Philip Carr-Gomm is our reference in figuring out how this whole process worked.

Since animals did not have symbols to represent them like the Ogham system did, the ovate relied on the sighting of the animal in real life. Typical of the druid system in general, the standard was confined to three animals sighted in a relatively short period of time. Either you went out to see your oracle or the ovate would do it for you. Unlike the Ogham process, this was much easier to define. Each animal's meaning was brief and to the point, so it made it much simpler to get a reading. However, because of this, it could also have a serious chance of being a hit or miss scenario.

Often the practice of an animal oracle was conducted for new kings. The ovates wanted to see what kind of leadership they could expect from how the wild life responded to the new leader. For example, the sighting of crows and ravens in an animal oracle is never a good sign. On the other hand, sighting an owl or a swan is an extremely good omen. Then you have everything in between.

There are twenty-nine animals in the general oracle practice according to Peter B. Ellis's research (*The Animal Oracle*). In the Welsh animal oracle system, four dragons are added. The dragons did not come into the system until after the fourth century, for obvious reasons (King Arthur).

Since the animal oracle system is relatively light compared to the tree Ogham, the messages gained from it are not as serious. In general, druids labelled the animal oracle as a process to heighten knowledge on a said issue, not really to foretell the future. However, they do not rule out what symbols the animals bring upon an issue. Like I said earlier, a crow is never a good sign in these cases.

So now I will reveal some of the typical animals the ovates had in their oracle, and at the end I will give a brief demo on how it was applied.

Black Bird is on the top of the oracle system. It represents the power of movement between the two worlds. It is the symbol of insight.

The Red Deer is also near the top of importance in the system. This animal represents abundance. It is an enchanted animal in both Ireland and Scotland. It symbolizes grace and femininity.

The Stag symbolizes pride and independence. For this symbol to have its best representation, it is preferred that it be seen between two trees. It means your divination comes from the other-world.

The Bear, once a common animal in Britain, was now extinct. It symbolizes power and sovereignty. As many will know, the bear was the characteristic symbol of King Arthur. It is the spiritual symbol of a warrior.

The Fox is well respected for its cunning. There are still foxes to be found in Britain. The fox represents cunning, diplomacy, and wildness. This symbol represents that the person is hard to work with.

The Cat represents guardianship and sensuality. Cats bring a quiet situation of observation. They symbolizes goodness on all fours.

The Boar represents the warrior spirit and leadership. Often Celtic helmets had boars on them, symbolizing warrior prowess. This animal represents wildness and raw power.

The Hawk is the symbol of nobility, recollection, and cleansing. Hawks are also associated with Beltane and thus the symbol of new beginnings. In Welsh mythology the hawk also represents quest, as was the case in the quest for the Holy Grail.

The Dog represents guidance, protection, and loyalty. Dogs are mentioned in just about all mythological stories of the British Isles, like Cu-Chulainn in the Tan Bo.

The Owl is the symbol of detachment, wisdom, and change—the change being from bad to good. This symbol is one of aloofness and the total silence of wisdom. This is definitely a good sign.

The Crane represents sweet knowledge from patience. From the patience comes perseverance. Religiously cranes are recognized as guardians to the other world with Mananann.

The Frog is the symbol of sensitivity, medicine, and hidden beauty. Being so close to water it is also associated with magical powers, for water is one of the four great elements. This is a solid symbol of a positive nature.

The Raven has two symbols; one of protection and one of a bad omen. In terms of protection, the meaning comes from the legend of Bran's head being buried in London. In terms of a bad omen, it is when it is seen at a battle site. The raven is associated with the goddess Morrigan.

The Swan is another powerful symbol. It represents the soul, beauty, and love. Dozens of love stories like *The Children of Lir* have numerous swans in them to demonstrate the point. Samhain has the symbol of the swan in it to show positive change.

The Wolf has a symbol not readily recognized, for many would suspect it to be a negative one, but it's not. The wolf represents intuition, learning, and a shadowy mystery in a good sense. It also represents inner strength and taking risks.

The Adder or snake, is the symbol of transformation and healing. It was adopted by the medical profession. On Gundestrup Cauldron, the snakes seen on it represent fertility.

The Eagle represents intelligence and courage. The eagle is recognized as the king of all birds. The time of the eagle is during the festival of Lughnasah. In Scotland, three eagle feathers are a sign of good luck. The eagle is on the same level as a salmon.

The Sow symbolizes generosity and nourishment, for obvious reasons. The sow was one of the leading food sources of the entire Celtic world. It is no wonder they were associated with plentiful and economic prosperity.

The Bull is a nice way to end it all. This great creature symbolizes strength, wealth, and potency. The bull in the Celtic culture has the highest economic value of anything. Having a bull in your oracle meant there was a great improvement to be experienced.

The Ram is symbolic of achievement, break-through, and sacrifice. It represents stability with no fears; all the characteristics of a powerful ram.

The Hare symbolizes rebirth, intuition, and balance. Hares are always a positive sign. Their month is March, which also accounts for fertility. In Ireland and Scotland for the longest time you did not eat a hare, for that was sign of bad luck.

The salmon is probably the most powerful symbol in the entire order, for it represents wisdom at its highest degree. Though it was fished for in ancient times, it was highly prized. This fish is mentioned in hundreds of Celtic legends like the Talisman.

As mentioned in the beginning, how it worked in application was in sets of three. You could go out into the wild and see what your chances were in seeing three animals or birds. Or as stated before, you could have a druid do it for you. Or in modern times, you can buy a box of animal oracle cards. The last being the simplest. Again, the trick is that the divination must be experienced in a short period of time, otherwise it is not valid. There is no absolute time frame, but at the same time you can't claim a divination over the length of a day either. I feel if you see three different creatures in the span of a few hours that's likely to be reasonable. Further, you cannot be looking for them. It must be natural. If when walking through a forest you just happen to see a crow, then that's legitimate and that's your first one. Then as you move along you really get lucky and see a deer, and that's your second one. Finally, if you come down to the water's edge and you spot a frog, well, that's your third one. Now put it all together:

Crow
Deer
Frog

Your Divination:

The Crow is grouped with the Raven;
so it could mean protection or a curse

The Deer, of course, is grouped with the Stag;
so, it could mean independence and freedom.

The Frog is straightforward, meaning
sensitivity and hidden beauty.

Now seeing that two of the signs are positive, that makes the first one (The Crow) positive as well. Druids tried to always keep things simple. After all, they were dealing with an illiterate society.

Thus, the overall divination was: Protection, Independence, and Hidden Beauty.

Something I did not mention before with the Ogham system is the wait time that went with every divination. Druids had a policy that you could only do one divination every new moon or in more modern times every thirty days. There was a practical side to this when you think about it. First, if the magic was real it would surely show itself within that time; if not, then enough time has gone by it's safe to try again. The druids, kind of like the Christians, believed in not pushing your luck; or trying the patience of the god(s). And especially when it came to a king you had to be very careful with the magic unless you wanted to lose your head.

CHAPTER 10

The Stone Circle and Passage Tombs

Beware of the unknown
Stay clear of the world's mysteries
Never sleep with your light off
Watch for the black cat
Close your ears to any screams
Do all this and life will sure to be a bore.

BRITISH – UNKNOWN - 1912

Stone circles and passage tombs are by far the most fascinating subjects in all of the ancient world of North West Europe. A vast majority of archaeologists like Michael Parker Pearson do not venture into saying who were the behind the building of these amazing structures. However, William Stukeley and Francis Pryor have no reservations about saying who it was.

Down in the most southwest corner of Ireland, in Castletown, County Cork in a very remote place called

Dereenatagh, is a stone circle, which was openly declared a druid construction. It was erected 2800 years ago. The reason for the decision was because the opening, lines up perfectly on August 1st with the rising sun (Lughnasah); something only druids would be associated with and no one else. Since the stone circle fits in with all the other circles around the British Isles it has an enormous impact in terms of verification.

This one little discovery means all the passage tombs and the stone circles now have to be examined individually. It is a monstrous undertaking, for on the continent in places like France and Spain, it is claimed there are over a thousand stone circles and passage tombs. In the United Kingdom it is claimed they have over 1,500, and in Ireland the authorities there go on the wild notion that there are over 3,000 stone circles and passage tombs. I personally have read up on about a hundred of them except for a very few dates to 2000 BC. Up until now most have been generally examined for the opening direction, which is not at all thorough. Once it is recognized the opening is certified in the east, the research stops. Only in a few examples like Stonehenge and Newgrange is the precise day is measured; the rest are only glanced at. Dereenatagh tells all the experts they had better go over their notes again. Should they find more openings line up on a different solstice date, then it would have a crushing impact on the whole druid question.

It's like with the true existence of King Arthur. If King Arthur did not exist, who then fought at the Battle of Badon? So far, the scholars have thoroughly examined Welsh Celtic society, but have not yet come up with a suitable replacement. Thus, we are left to say Arthur was the one. The same analysis can be applied to the druids. If there were a more advanced people to guide the Bronze Age People in building the stone circles, the scholars have yet to come up with a name. In the archaeological digs that Michael Parker Pearson has done it goes without question that the Bronze Age People onto themselves did not have the natural engineering skills to have built Stonehenge. It would have shown in their home and tool building apparatuses, but it does not. The average person built crude homes and used animal antlers as tools. Hardly a sign of sophistication. Therefore, it is unquestionable that they were led by a more advanced populous, and no one can name any except the druids.

Remember it was from Pliny the Elder we learned that the druids had very sophisticated mathematical skills. The implication is that they could very well have performed the task as directing engineers.

Before we start getting into all the interesting details of the stone circles and passage tombs, what has to be noted right off the top is that what is still seen today only represents likely two-thirds of what once existed. Sadly, a lot of history has been lost. From Richard Hayman's book *Riddle In Stone* and Peter Clayton's *Guide to the Archaeological Sites of Britain,* a lot of information has been provided on the extent of the destruction to the stone circles and the passage graves. Apparently, there were four major periods of destruction. The first one happened between 600 and 1100 AD. During this time, Christianity was trying to get a hold on England. From the writings of Saint Iltud, Saint Samson, and Bede the Venerable, it is claimed a number of stone circles were taken down. The second era happened in the late 1600s and carried on till circa 1720. This was probably the worst period of all. England and Wales suffered the most. An estimated more than 200 circles were dismantled. Avebury and Stonehenge suffered the most in this time frame. The reason for the destruction was due to an economic boom when they needed land for building.

The third happened in the early 1800s. Here there are no numbers but the word "substantial" was used to describe the number of stones that were taken down. It was in this period Scotland suffered the most. Finally, between 1901 and 1950 it was claimed a "limited amount of destruction" of circles and passage graves took place. I think the British were now trying to use words that made the damage appear not as bad as it really was.

I did a comparison between Ireland and Britain to come up with a probable number of how many circles were dismantled in the time frame noted. Ireland today has around 2,000 stone circles and passage graves. I would suspect that Britain, being a larger country, now has around 1500 circles and passage graves but would be at least equal to Ireland, meaning Britain suffered a minimum loss of 500 circles and passage graves. Seeing Brittany in France has still around 1000 standing stones and passage graves left, and they too suffered the same kind of destruction, I estimate they must have suffered around 300 circles destroyed. The likely overall destruction is estimated to be around a thousand in an 800-year period. If accurate this tells us just how much more of the land was originally covered in stones.

Stone Circle

John Aubrey, William Stukeley, and William Borlase discovered that one of the reasons for so many circles was because the burial grounds were just part of a much larger ceremonial setup. Avebury was the first. It had a long procession of a stone walkway leading to the Avebury stone circles and then continuing farther on to a minor stone circle. From a distance it looked like a huge stone-lined snake. Alfred Watkins was the first to rediscover this point in 1921 with his Lockyer Stonehenge Triangle. Here he proved that not only is there a local ceremonial pathway around the stones, like at Avebury, but that it extends for several miles into the countryside. He believes that Stonehenge is intricately connected with Avebury and beyond. Grahame Clark in his book, *Prehistoric England* notes a similar discovery with the Ickneild Way, which starts in Norfolk and extends into Canbridgeshire. Along this route is a series of stone circles and burial mounds that all appear to be connected. In more recent times it uncovered that there was a walkway that started about two miles north of Stonehenge at a place called Harington Hill and wound its way along the Avon river. Francis Pryor uncovered up on the Orkney Islands that the famed Callanish Stone Circle also has two ceremonial walkways; one locally around the stone circle and another that extends almost across the whole island and connects with a series of smaller stone circles. From these discoveries what was learned is that the burying ceremonies were an elaborate affair. No doubt the pagan priest (likely druid) had enormous importance. The verification it was likely a druid is from comparing the enormous burial ritual importance to the level of importance that Julius Caesar wrote about them. It seems to match nicely. Caesar said the druid was the centre of Celtic society and all things centred around them. Stonehenge, Mike Parker Pearson says, was a colossal project with the evidence showing that people came from all around. The pottery found there is from all over England, Scotland, and Ireland.

As mentioned, many of the stones have been taken down and only a dozen or so remain as a reminder of the once fantastic walkways. We are lucky in a sense that people like William Stukeley did drawings of the stones when many of them were still up. This tells of how much emphasis there must have been on the burial ceremonies. Mike Parker Pearson even discovered that not only were they enormous ceremonies, but they were held on two very important days of the year; the winter and summer solstices. When I come to detailing the building of Stonehenge, I will get more into this point.

If you were to include all the stone circles and passage graves from Britany, England, Wales, Scotland, and Ireland, which roughly accounts for close to 5000 sites, it is readily apparent there is a similar design pattern to them all. First, as many people around the world know, is that just about all of them either point or line up to the east. The easterly direction is to the winter and summer solstice for the most part. Second, it was discovered by Borlase that when it comes to the stone circles the vast majority of them are in prime number count. The ones that aren't, scholars believe, is because some of the stones have fallen or have been removed. Next it was found that a substantial number of them have a burial of a cremated body in the centre. In Scotland they know for a fact it was deliberate. As mentioned before, the passage graves they found are designed to have set number of skeletons in them and they never go over that figure. Also, especially during the Beaker People period, bodies were always put in a fetal position. During the Urnfield People era, a substantial number of the bodies in the graves were cremated. Overall, it is generally accepted that both the passage graves and the stone circles represent the same thing—life after death. The reason for that is the burials were celebrated on one of the two solstices and there was always found an urn of food or drink in a passage grave. The solstices are believed to be when the dead come back to visit the living. Lastly, the Tristan stone carvings are a universal symbol whenever it is found in the chambers. This is only a few examples of this type of pattern discovered.

Stone Carving Tristan

If we start with the Man-on-ton stone down deep in southwest Cornwall we can begin to see how much druid-associated superstition has been built into the stone circles. Man-on-ton is a single round stone with a huge hole in the centre. It is approximately three metres high and the opening, of course, faces east. This keeps to all the standards with stone monuments. The stone sits out in an open field and its real purpose is not known. Archaeologists date the stone to 2500 BC. The first recordings of people's activities around this stone are from the sixth century. The opening was said to have had magic to it. If you were ill, crawling through the hole three times would cure you of your illness. There is no evidence this ever really worked. However, to this very day people continue to practice the ritual, whether they actually believe in the magic or are simply having a little fun. The thing here to note is the number three. Three is the most powerful number in the druid world. As mentioned earlier, the carvings on the Tristan stones are in three circles.

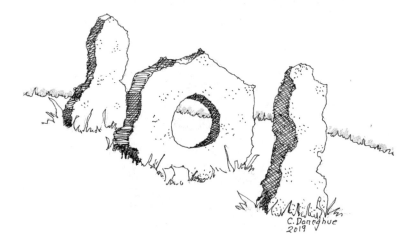

Man-On-Ton Stone

As we move away from Cornwall and enter Gloustershire we come across another stone similar in nature to the Man-on-ton stone; "The Stone of Gloustershire." Again, here is a stone that sits in the middle of a field and has a rather large gaping hole in it. This one is only large enough for a small child to pass through. Sure enough, local records tell of various people through the centuries passing their babies through the hole for two purposes. The first was to prevent disease and the second was if the child was ill, to cure him/her of the illness. And, like the Man-on-ton stone, the ritual was that the child had to be passed through the hole three times. Here local authorities have no reservations in accusing the druids for being responsible for this superstitious practice.

This now leads us to some of the research on these continued pagan practices concerning the stones. Numerous names come up on the topic such as Saint Sampson, Saint Iltud, Saint David, Bede, and Nennius. These people wrote extensive accusations against the druids for the pagan practices that were still going on in the fifth century in Wales and Cornwall. But how could that be when it is commonly accepted that the Romans killed all the druids in Anglesey in AD 61? The fact is they did not get them all, many survived. Anglesey was just a large meeting place for many druids but not the end-all for them. The Romans fooled themselves into believing they were all annihilated and many a British historian today has gone along with it. The result of this event was that those druids who survived the slaughter went underground or escaped to Ireland and Pictland. Once the Romans left Britannia in AD 410, the druids easily re-emerged again. First accounts of their reappearance surface as early as AD 475 in Llandaff, Wales. As we know, in Ireland and Scotland records of their existence go back even further like with Saint Patrick in 435 AD. From the writings and legends of the Irish king, Cormac MacAirte in 260 AD we find Ireland was crawling with druids—there were over a thousand. We find out this number was confirmed at the famous Drumceat Council in AD 475 with king Áed mac Ainmuirech. So, the belief that all the druids were killed in Anglesey is sheer nonsense.

From this opening observation comes the question, were the rituals being practiced at the stone circles only at the arrival of the Celts; or was it going on much earlier? The answer to that question actually gets revealed when we start to move to Stonehenge itself.

The Avebury stone circles just North West of Stonehenge are by far the most interesting site when it comes to druids.

Avebury was first examined at length by the famous John Aubrey, circa 1670. It was then studied by an equally famous antiquarian, William Stukeley, circa 1730. Both men wrote extensive documents on their research and each concluded that the engineering of the stone circles was done by none other than the druids. Barry Cunliffe and few more of his contemporaries have dismissed Aubrey and Stukeley. In Barry's book, *A Brief History of druids*, he claims there was a revival movement of the druid cult going on when Aubrey and Stukeley were conducting their studies in the 18th century, and that it's likely they got caught up in that. The only problem with Barry's argument is that he got the time frame and location of the revival wrong. There was a druid revival, but it did not happen in Britain; but in Brittany, France in the late 1700s and really it didn't take off until the middle of the 1800s. This suggests that what Stukeley and Aubrey studied at Avebury was in fact built by the original order of druids.

When William Stukeley examined the Avebury Stone Circles, he reported that he came across actual druids practicing their arts. His writing indicates he had a physical encounter with them and from it he concluded they were the engineers of the circles. Though John Aubrey doesn't state it in his work, but certainly implies to having had the same experience. From that experience he too concluded the druids had been the stone circle engineers.

One of the most interesting points to come from Aubrey and Stukeley's documents was their theory on the purpose of the stone circles. Both men found that as far back as the seventeenth century, observing the celestials was for the purpose of honouring ancestors. Since few, if anyone, today will read these writings, modern scholars have decided they can get away with claiming Michael Parker Pearson is the original discoverer of the ritual purpose of honouring the ancestors. This is another falsehood that has become widely accepted – a very unfortunate circumstance for Aubrey and Stukeley. It's similar to how the public is led to believe Christopher Columbus discovered the Americas when in fact it was the Vikings who were first.

Both Stonehenge and the Avebury Stone circles are/were surrounded with burial mounds. In the seventeenth century there were hundreds upon hundreds of them. Since that time just about all them have been excavated and removed. It was after this point that William Stukeley deduced their purposes. You see, it is a major part of Michael Parker Pearson's excavation Stukeley is missing in his final observation. When Pearson did his dig in 2005, all the burial mounds were gone when he drew the conclusion about the cremation urns being the central point of the ritual activity. This is hardly accurate. In 1754 Richard Colt Hoare and William Cunningham made an inventory of all the artifacts and riches that were being taken from the two locations. They realized that so much had been taken from the sites already that the government authorities should be called in to control the digs. One of the more horrifying aspects of the amateur digs that was going on was that gold was being found and sold on the antiquity markets. In Richard Hayman's book *Riddles of the Stone* he points out from Hoare and Cunningham's observations alone that the interpretation of Avebury and Stonehenge is clearly missing enormous evidence necessary to modern understanding, because we are only accepting contemporary research from the two sites. There is no doubt the museums are filled with artifacts found at the two circles, but no one is disclosing their source. What this tells us is that the major events on the solstices were not the only time celestial activities took place here.

As far as William Stukeley was concerned Avebury was still in operation when it came to the druids. They came out two times a day; once in the early morning and once late at night, especially when the moon or stars were out. Only because we have telescopes today are we able to understand what Stukeley was reporting about the druid activity. He wasn't sure, nor could he confirm that what the druids were pointing at in the sky was accurate. He could only take their word for it. Let's face it, Stukeley was not an astronomer. We know now from research done on the Mesopotamians that people like the druids who studied the skies could tell the difference between stars and planets with the naked eye. This is not magic by today's standards but certainly was in the time of William Stukeley. Many a British historian surmised from the way Stukeley wrote his report that he was enamoured with the druids. Contemporary scholars can understand the reason he was so impressed with the druids. The technology to define what they were doing simply didn't exist.

At this point a moment must be taken to get an idea of what Avebury looked like in its heyday. The layout was very unique. It had one very large circle of stones with two smaller circles inside it. The outer circle was encased by a large, circular mound, that still exists today. There are no stone circles of this design to be found anywhere else in Europe. William observed that only one of the small circles at any given time was used, meaning there was some kind of special significance to the two circles. Further, whether it was night or morning determined what circle was used. William Stukeley never did find out what the significance of this practice was, and it turns out we may never know for the druids have not returned to the place since the destruction began in the middle of the eighteenth century. Britain was going through an economic boom and building was happening all across the country. Avebury was one of the focal points and in the process of construction, they took down hundreds of the stones to make way for new homes. Also, according to Stukeley when news got out that several of the burial mounds had gold in them, a gold rush started taking place. Burial mounds got dug up all over. It is estimated hundreds of ancient sites were pilfered. A contemporary author by the name of John Clayton (*Guide to Stone Circles*) claims the destruction was even more extensive than William Stukeley reported. Clayton feels thousands of stone circles were dismantled and that an equal number of burial mounds were infiltrated by poachers.

THE AVEBURY HENGE

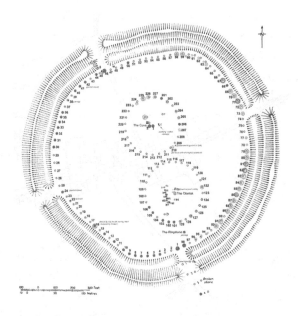

Avebury Stone Circle

What did result from this event was that starting in the late nineteenth century, druids – likely from the revival movement, moved their activities to Stonehenge. As I understand it, they still practice their arts here on the winter and summer solstices. No one has taken the time to examine these practices to see if there are any similarities to the ones followed in the sixteenth century.

From here on, we are going to travel all the way up to the Orkney Islands of Scotland. An amazing discovery was made here by the archaeologist Francis Pryor in 2010, which confirmed William Stukeley's "The Avebury (stone) Snake." The site that Francis Pryor examined was called the Ring of Brodgar. There are only a few huge megalith stones in this circle. This, Pryor found out is only a starting point to a much larger set up of stones. From Brodgar, a string of stones leads to a path to another stone circle known as the Stinith Circle. Again, there are only a few stones left standing from the original assembly. However, Pryor discovered it doesn't stop here—the trail continues for yet another mile. This trail/path ends at a place called Maeshowe. What was discovered is that all these circles are connected. It was a huge ceremonial path for the purpose of honouring ancestors. In fact, based on the evidence, the ceremony must have taken place several times a year and culminated on the winter solstice.

Maeshowe is a stone structure built on the location of what was someone's home centuries earlier. The home is symbolic. It is surrounded by a series of fire pits, which archaeologists feel were once also wooden homes. Here are buried the cremated remains of people who likely once lived here. The ritual is quite different compared to Stonehenge, but the meaning is the same. People died and were buried where they lived. Once all the members of the family passed away, the home was abandoned. Over time other people would come back and start to build stone frames around the former home, and eventually they made a shrine of the place. The former inhabitants were now regarded as the ancestors and were to be given special honour and asked for protection. Maeshowe is another very different passage grave, in that the opening faces west. It is exactly set up that the light of the setting sun of the winter solstice enters the tomb, not the rising summer solstice as is the common practice with all the other burial sites.

What was revealed in all these places is that their central purpose has nothing to do with the stars. The stars only act as an amplification of the main function of the burial ceremony. A lot of people are fixated on the concept that the stone-circles principle is that of a celestial centre. They couldn't be further from the truth. The druids were conducting rituals to celebrate the dead and their practices are confirmed with what has been uncovered in 2500 BC. It was from this new research it has been realized that the druids were the source of what was going on in Britain for the last 5,000 years. When you compare the notes of John Aubrey and William Stukeley with those of Francis Pryor and Michael Parker Pearson, you see right away the similarity in time. The druids were conducting the same ceremonies in the eighteenth century as was confirmed with the rituals done in the Neolithic Age.

Now to see what the research and practices were at Stonehenge and once more compare them with those of Brodgar and Avebury.

There was many a person as early as King Henry VIII, who lightly examined Stonehenge, but the first serious study was done by John Webb at the request of King Charles I (1640). Ancient history was by and large relied upon by such people like Nennius, Bede, and even Geoffrey Monmouth. John Webb somehow concluded Stonehenge was built by the Vikings. So, even with the first serious look at the circles, it too was pretty far fetch like everything else that was being considered at the time.

The second serious study of Stonehenge was done by a John Aubrey in 1663. By contrast, Aubrey conducted a thorough examination and concluded that Stonehenge, like Avebury, was engineered by the druids. He dated Stonehenge as being built in the fifth century BC. Though completely wrong, he was taking us in the right direction. The circles are definitely much older than the Viking Age. He was the first to identify that the druids had been/were conducting ceremonies here. As mentioned, he leads us to believe in having had an actual exchange with them in which confirmed his observations. Unlike Stukeley, he's careful not to fully commit his evidence as real proof.

The third person to do a serious study of Stonehenge that went on for years was, of course, (again) the great William Stukeley in 1730. He did one of the earliest maps of the place and we learned from him some of the first terms to describe the arrangements of the stones, like "stone lintel." Again, we find that Stukeley didn't hesitate to identify the druids as both the engineers and ceremony conductors at the site. Like Aubrey, he felt the celestial ceremonies were connected to the burial rituals. The specifics he did not quite figure out, though he did write a rather detailed account of his observations, and oddly enough, he came desperately close to putting it all together. Like his predecessor, he concluded that Stonehenge was built in the fifth century BC. Once more with this site, Stukeley's conclusions were confirmed by Pearson in his 2005 excavation. The observations on the ceremonies by both men are uncanny in that they are exactly the same. However, Pearson will not commit to the conclusion that the druids were the priests of their time.

I suppose this is what the rub is. Two identical researches take place and one source will identify the persons responsible while the other will not.

As mentioned before, Stukeley found that Stonehenge was surrounded by hundreds of burial sites. He excavated a substantial number of them and stumbled upon the fact that many were royal graves filled with gold artifacts. Of course, this discovery caused an instant sensation and every amateur in the land came racing to the site. Due to that frenzy, the archaeological damage was irreparable. Where once stood hundreds of mounds was all level ground leaving a nothing more than a barren, flat field, which remains to this very day. What is unfortunate about this is that it is all kept hidden from modern research. People today are under the impression that what you see at Stonehenge is the way it actually was; that it was flat and with only one structure. This couldn't be further from the truth. If you should ever read the research done by William Stukeley and go over his drawings you will see the area was once covered in mounds. Since the sixteenth century, all the burial sites have been excavated and then flattened. Also, from Michael Parker Pearson's excavation in 2005 it was learned that at the north end of Stonehenge were literary hundreds of foundations to temporary houses. Two thousand years ago, this place would have looked like a huge, wooden city. Most definitely, what we see on Salisbury Plain today is only a tiny fraction of what was here even 300 years ago.

The next person to do a thorough examination of Stonehenge was a Dr. Johnson in 1783. With no hesitation he also concluded the structure was engineered by the druids. On top of this he was the first to date the construction to around 2000 BC. Therefore, the idea of the druids being involved with Stonehenge is now expanded to three researchers.

In 1812, Sir Richard Colt did an extensive excavation in and around Stonehenge. He became the fourth person to conclude the construction had something to do with druids. So, the druid concept is still with us. Remarkably, despite the previous frenzies, Colt was able to find a few more burial sites. He too determined the site was built around 2000 BC. An unfortunate result of his work was that a fair bit of damage was done to the stones due to all his excessive digging. It is said he dug so deep around the stones that some fell over.

It wasn't until 1883 that the druid and Celt concepts were finally abandoned, and the prehistoric concept was introduced. Dr. W. Long first came up with the theory that Stonehenge was built by an -unknown people- of a much earlier period. Whoever they were, they were definitely not Celts. He does make an interesting observation that once again joins Stukeley and Pearson's research together by tying the burial practices in with astronomy. What Dr. Long didn't expect in his research was that what he wrote had too many similarities to the Celtic practices of Samhain. In his attempt to separate the druids from Stonehenge, he only ended up making the site completely associated to the Celts. Perhaps he should have had an editor go over his work.

Even though Long inadvertently messed up the identity of the people, he was the first to find antlers and realize they were the principle digging tool for the construction. Also, while everybody else was going for the gold, he was the first to take a proper look at the pottery of the site and he determined that it came not only from Britain but Ireland as well. This discovery was verified by Pearson's excavation in 2005.

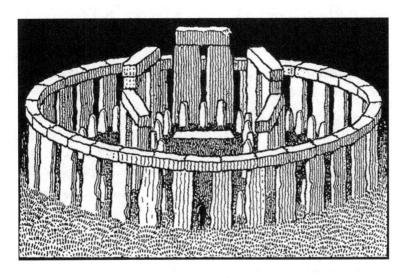

Stonehenge

The next big date of evolutionary significance was in 1939, with researchers Stuart Piggott and Richard Atkinson. These two did yet another major excavation that went on for an amazing period of time and ended in 1956. What was remarkable about this research was the discovery that Stonehenge was built in three stages over a period of 500 years. The first stage was nothing more than an enormous, completely circular mound with an interior circle of fifty small stones. The second stage was the mound with its east and west ends cut away, with two marking stones on the outside of the east end of the circle. These stones have been become known as the Heel Stone and the Slaughter Stone. They gave the first indicators of the astronomical signifi-cance of the rising sun on the summer and winter solstice.

The third stage is what we know of the structure today; the enormous stone structure with the lintels. Also, there was the discovery of three distinct types of stones that made up the structure; Sarsen stones, Blue Stones, and one Green Stone for the altar stone.

Richard Atkinson made probably the most amazing discovery for all the stone circles throughout Europe. He discovered the cremains of a body in the centre of the stone circle. It was found that nearly all the stone circles throughout Europe had human remains buried in the centre of each of their circles. In all the cases, the body buried was a young male. It is believed it may have been a special blessing or symbol of protection for the site. Some believe it may have been an offering. Have to admit it was an astonishing discovery.

And the next amazing discovery of the structure was the preciseness of its construction and its accurate alignment to astronomical events. Archaeologists were able to confirm the Celtic and Lunar Calendars. The days were exactly measured. Next was the confirmation of the fundamental measuring unit of 20.8 inches, which was first discovered by William Stukeley. That unit told everybody that the engineering behind the building of the structure was far more advanced than they would have ever imagined. Very sophisticated thinking went into the building of Stonehenge, even though the tools used were unbelievably primitive, like the deer antlers. From this discovery the thinking again went back to druids since they were the only people known to have such advanced lines of thinking; so, we are coming full circle. First, we say it was the druids, then we say it is not the druids, and then finally we say again it was the druids. It would seem the scholars can't make up their minds.

You see, as much as they have tried to uncover some unknown, super-intelligent, shaman people who may have really engineered Stonehenge and all the other megaliths, they keep coming up empty handed. The only people that even come close to this advanced line of thinking in architectural design are the druids.

Now, as much as this is going to seem redundant, it has to be mentioned one more time to complete the picture of Stonehenge's secrets. The 2005 excavation did uncover things that were not known before. The big discovery Pearson made was that Stonehenge was a much bigger site than ever anticipated. The Woodhenge uncovered a kilometer up the Avon River revealed this is where the ceremony likely started. Pearson confirmed Stukeley's findings that the place was indeed a burial site on a massive scale. The astronomical importance did, in fact, tie in with the burial ceremonies. William Stukeley was vindicated. What is ironic is that it was declared a new discovery when it wasn't. The good thing that came of Pearson's excavation was putting to bed for once and for all that Stonehenge was purely an astronomical altar where the druids worshipped their gods. That was a point of view that persisted for decades and since so many knew so little of the druids, it stuck.

These discoveries extended past Stonehenge, to Ireland's Newgrange, and confirmed the theories at Scotland's Brodgar as well. In all of these places the ceremonies were the same. The focus was on the ancestors and the protection they provided the community. In Ireland, as many know, it goes even one step further. On the festival of Samhain not only do they ask their ancestors to protect them but to come out and walk amongst the living. And it is important to note this festival did not originate with the Celts as is the common understanding. What is kind of amusing is how Michael Parker Pearson, who drew so many associations to the druids; won't admit to it officially. When questioned on it, he chooses his words well. He hints that maybe whoever the people were who engineered Stonehenge may have passed on their knowledge to the druids and that is why they know so much about the circles today. Once more, even *he* had no intuition as to who the strange Neolithic engineers were, who ended up passing on their knowledge.

The physical building of Stonehenge:

To start with, here are some fundamental statistics on the structure of Stonehenge. As everybody knows, Stonehenge was built in three stages. The second stage, which involved the stones, took around fifty or more years to complete. The Sarsen stones came from a quarry not far from the site and the Blue stones are said to have come from the south of Wales. Stonehenge is a series of circles. The first ring is the outer circle mound. It is approximately 120 metres in diameter. Next are the Aubrey holes. These holes are where the blue stones first sat, though they were later moved inside the Sarsen stones. These holes are measured at roughly 110 metres in diameter. Coming in closer now to the actual first Sarsen lintel stone circle, the diameter is 70 metres in diameter. The famed Blue stone circle is 40 metres in diameter and finally the enormous Horseshoe stone circle is 30 meters in diameter. There are four sets of stones. The Sarsen outer ring stones are five to six metres in height and weigh roughly 26 tons. Next are the much smaller blue stones, of which around 50 or so are still standing from the original 110. They are two to three meters high and weight approximately four tons each. The enormous Horseshoe stones in the middle are 7.3 metres in height and each weigh about 35 tons. There is no data on the green altar stone, but it is estimated to be around 20 tons. By the inside mound there are two stones and two large potholes that line up on the compass at north, south, east, and west exactly, which verifies its engineers had it line up to the winter and summer solstice sun. There are two stones that mark the entrance. The Heel stone is first and the farthest stone is the Slaughter stone. These stones are estimated to weigh around eight tons each. Lastly, there is the ring of graves that sits just inside the mound circle. Most are filled with cremation ashes and some have bones. There are around a hundred burial sites and only one body had personal effects with him. None of the bodies were female. It is an academic guess that these bodies were likely very important people, but not necessarily of royal status. William Stukeley was able to confirm this point in his studies. He found hundreds of graves with caches of gold jewelry on the outside of the mound circle, which verified the burials were of royal status.

You now have an idea what the whole structure basically looked like and its size. The stones that are still in existence represent only about 60% of what was originally there. Many of the stones have either fallen down or were removed in the seventeenth century, during the great economic boom.

The tools and the engineering feat of the stone structure are obviously what people are most curious about.

Here again we find we are dependent on two people for these answers since they have the most up-to-date data on the place; Francis Pryor and Michael Parker Pearson. In Pearson's 2005 dig, something found in unusual quantities, which had never been seriously considered before, was stone balls with an indent to them. It was found the shape fit comfortably in a person's hand. Your fingers naturally fall into the indent of the stone. Thus, it came as no surprise this was the main tool used for cutting and shaping the stone blocks. The stone balls came in two sizes; one large and one small. It was concluded the large one was used for rough cutting and the small one for refining. If you are wondering how they worked, it was quite simple. Holding the stone in hand, they slammed it hard against the surface of the rock slab. The continuous pounding chipped away the surface. After a very lengthy period they eventually carved out the shape they needed. The next tool, which was found in enormous quantities, was deer antlers. Archeologists surmise this was the tool used for digging and scraping. Animal hip bones with wooden handles were also found, and they were interpreted as a crude form of shovel. The most amazing discovery was the three-inch round balls. Only a few were found but they connected with a discovery made in Scotland where hundreds of these stone balls were found. It was from these that it was learned that the transportation of the stone slabs did not happen on a series of logs but on something more like ball-bearing conveyers. The experiments by engineers in Scotland confirmed that this method took far less manpower to move a stone weighting up to twenty tons.

Neolithic Stone Balls

This bring us to our next big point. What kind of manpower was used in building the colossal project? Archeological digs in the late '80s found that where Stonehenge stands was once an area of thick forest. They also found, which was later confirmed in 2005, that the place had a huge habitation of houses. This means space was very limited. Further, Pearson observes that during the solstice festival there was an added influx of people, who built temporary structures in the area as well. This led to the conclusion that the workforce building Stonehenge was not as massive as many contemporary historians believe was the case. A historian by the name of Gerald S. Hawkins (*Stonehenge Decoded*) figures there were not more than 5,000 at best, who were involved in the construction, and maybe as few as 2,000. Tongue-in-cheek, he figures that if the place was engineered by the druids, the skill level would have been fairly high and the masses of people were not necessary. He drew that same conclusion from studying the papers of the Greek historian, Pliny, who noted the druid's knowledge in mathematics.

As mentioned before, the large Sarsen stones came from a quarry where Marlborough Downs sits now. The Blue stones came from the southern perimeter of Wales. The exact location is still under debate, but scholars are confident the stones did come from Wales. It still has not been determined where the Green altar stone came from. The stones were pounded out of the ground with the hand rocks described above. Archeologists found huge gravel grades where they figured the ball-bearing ramps were laid for the Sarsen stones and this is how they were transported to the construction site. An engineer from the University of Wales determined the Blue Stones were transported by two twenty-five-foot dugout log boats strapped together with cross railings and the stones placed on the rails. Dugout boats were the common mode of water transportation in 2000 BC.

Now we have determined the most likely methods used to transport the stones. How they were refined and assembled is next. The Sarsen stones have what is described as cross lintels on top of them. These stones have bumps on them and the uprights have indents to accommodate the bumps. The engineering term for this is male and female stones. Thus, we know the lintels were not just placed across the top, they were designed to be permanently fixed in place. The precision of all this is uncanny. The ground surface from west to east has a slight downgrade of 1.5 degrees. And, going from north to south, it has a downgrade of 1.9 degrees. Yet at the top of the lintels is perfectly level. This is matched by the fact many of the stones in themselves are of different heights; in some cases with as much as one foot difference. This means each upright stone was individually crafted into place. The thing about that is, not only was there a different downgrade going on the X-Y axis but also on the diagonal. Someone had to have been directing the work for this kind of precision to be taking place.

This comes at last to understanding how the manpower was used. A substantial number of British historians have taken the position that Stonehenge was built by mob consensus. But the everyday structure of people's homes in around Salisbury at the time show the level of technical capability was extremely limited. Homes were crudely build with thatched roofs. Nothing in their design showed the average person had any unusually gifted skills. This leads us to the conclusion that only a select group of people could have engineered such a project. Gerald Hawkins comes up with the same observation I do, since there are no written records from whoever really masterminded Stonehenge. The only people who seemed to have an above-average knowledge about Stonehenge, both in its construction and use, were druids. Hawkins, unlike Stukeley, won't fully commit to this idea, but also says he can't rule it out either. He says when you read Julius Caesar's accounts of druids it stands to reason they are the only possible people who could have designed and managed the construction of Stonehenge. Caesar points out the druids had a near-mystical ability to control the masses. Everybody listened to them—even the kings. Their slightest wishes were obeyed without question. It is only from this capability that the refined quality and engineering of Stonehenge could have been accomplished. Anything less and the crudity would be instantly noted. One thing is certain, the design engineering of Stonehenge is at a high level of precision. Only people of unusual ability could have accomplished such a project. The idea that Stonehenge was built by mass consensus is nothing short of an absurdity.

I guess at this point a brief understanding of the people who physically built Stonehenge should be attempted. This should be a straightforward statement on this point, but as I have found out it is anything but. It is firmly agreed-upon that Stonehenge was built in several stages between 2800 BC and 2100 BC. The structure with the huge Sarsen Stones, in particular, is recognized to have been put up between 2200-2100 BC and was the last stage. What I have found is that the study of the people of the pre-Bronze Age has not been given enough research, and that there are people like Gerald Hawkins who got it all backwards. The latest research shows the earliest "culture" group that existed in Britain was the "Bell-Beaker Culture." Since the "Urnfield Culture" didn't appear until after 2100 BC, they had nothing to do with the construction. Therefore, going by the dates, it would seem the Beaker People were the ones who built Stonehenge. It should also be noted the dominant age in terms of the construction was the Bronze Age. This means a lot when it comes to many of the burial artifacts. We can verify the period in which they were made.

The Pan Beaker Culture was an industrious, agricultural people. How they got their name was the design of their clay pottery. A substantial amount of it is of a beaker design. These people lived in rectangular houses and were one of the first cultures to make woolen cloth with a loom. They lived a fairly peaceful existence in a structured society. Evidence shows they had chiefs of their communities. Based on their diet and lifestyle, archeologists have concluded that individuals lived much longer than the Celts did. It is estimated the average life expectancy was sixty years while for the Celts it did not exceed forty-five years. This tells you the harmony and cohesiveness of the Beaker Culture was at a much higher level than that of later cultures that arrived in Britain. Gerald Hawkins claims from his research that there is a substantial amount of evidence of arrowheads, gold, bronze, wooden tools, and an excess of pottery. The pottery use was far more varied in design than any other culture, supporting the argument they were more advanced than those that came after them. Therefore, combined with the dates and this understanding of the people themselves, it now seems more than likely the Beaker Culture people built Stonehenge

The research that Michael Parker Pearson did in 2005 revealed that the ceremony around the burial at Stonehenge was an elaborate festival that went on over several days. The excess of animal bones (primarily pigs) clearly indicates it was a huge feast. Pearson is convinced burying the dead had an enormous importance to the Beaker Culture. The point here is how important this ceremony was to the people and therefore explains why they went to so much trouble building Stonehenge in the first place. As was explained the druids are the only ones by name how had an in-depth knowledge of the stars. Further, it's been confirmed they had a superior knowledge of mathematics.

Putting the two together makes them the most likely group to have masterminded Stonehenge; and its purpose.

Also, it has to be remembered when Michael did his excavation, the hundreds of burial mounds that circled outside Stonehenge had long since been leveled. Though he had managed to come up with new data on the grounds, it still fell seriously short, because so much of the original site had been removed. By not recognising this he is missing a substantial portion to his research. Had he saw the ground in its original form as Stukeley did, you know he would have had quite a different conclusion.

Further, the idea that the place was also used for sacrifices or offerings was firmly dismissed in the 2005 dig. As mentioned numerous times now, Stonehenge was a centre for honouring the dead and nothing else. The Beaker Culture very much believed in an afterlife; a tradition that was passed down to the Celts when they arrived.

From all this we can now see why the elaborate effort went into the construction, and why so much effort was exerted in building it. When the enormous slabs came to their final spot, they were taken to a place just south of the construction site. Here the precision stage would begin. The stones were measured, and the adjoining stone would have been carved exactly so the two would fit together. Then they were taken over to the construction site itself, where likely with a wooden bridge scaffold system, the uprights were placed in the ground and the lintels placed on top of them. The druids/engineers knew exactly how big this was going to be. It was not just an act of grandiosity. As numerous scholars have now fully agreed upon, everything centred on the precise activities of stars, the moon, and the sun. The sun and the moon had to exactly behave with the structure.

This was not a hit or miss venture. When William Stukeley found that the foundation measurement was 20.8 inches and it has still not changed since then, it is pretty much a confirmation right there that it was all fully calculated. No doubt there was a single mind that was guiding all the rest.

Common sense seems to dictate that the structure started from the inside and worked itself to the outside. Therefore, the green stone altar was first and the Sarsen stones on the outer ring were last. However, some scholars feel the Blue stones may have been last because they were there before the Sarsen stones came. Once more, it was John Aubrey who discovered the Blue stones previously lined the far dirt mound before being brought inside the Sarsen stone structure.

As we know today, when it was completed the precision of the place was found to be perfect. The two big dates at Stonehenge were undeniably the summer and winter solstices. The sun rises and falls lined up with the centre two horseshoe stones exactly. Standing at the Heel stone, the diameter of the outside ring works perfectly with the setting moons. The way the stars and the moon play over the years, the number of Blue Stones confirm the complete cycle is 29.8 years. The druids somehow knew it was not a perfect number in the lunar cycle. Also, people like Aubrey Burl, in his book *A Brief history of Stonehenge*, discovered that November 1st (Samhain), August 1st (Lughnasah), February 1st (Imbolc) and May 1st (Beltane) are precisely measured as well. That brings out one of the greatest pieces of reinforcing evidence that the druid had to been involved.

The academics found that everything about the place lines up with the celestial bodies; the stars, the moon and the sun. Further, the Blue Stones measured the days of the year. Lastly, the big feature was the Heel stone at the east side of the complex. They know it lines up perfectly with the far west side of the circle on the summer and winter solstices. From all the various astronomical features of the place, it wasn't hard to figure out that whatever activity was going here it was completely tied in with the heavens. Obviously, with the hundreds of burials both inside and out, scholars knew there was a connection. In a manner of speaking, even in the Christian faith we still put the two subjects together when burying a loved one. It's not just a case of burying someone and walking away. We are hoping that God looks favourably on the deceased.

It has now been proven that the ceremony for the burial was an enormous event going over several days. People would gather at the Woodhenge up the Avon river. Here it is believed a huge feast took place. Also, the final preparations for the deceased were made as well. There were these large, wooden platforms where if any of the bodies still had flesh on them, they were placed here to naturally decay. What was left was cremated and placed in urns. When everybody was ready, a massive procession would start, going down the west side of the bank of the Avon towards Stonehenge itself. Of course, it was led by the priestess. The people of lower rank in the community were expected to empty their urns of ash into the river as the procession proceeded. The people of higher rank waited till they got to the site itself. The timing had to be perfect. As Pearson found out, there was a stone structure of five uprights marking the ascent to Stonehenge itself. Here is where everybody made a sharp right turn, went up a slight gradient, and moved west.

When everybody got to the crest they would have witnessed something quite remarkable—the setting sun coming through the centre of the upright pillars of the Horseshoe Sarsen stones. From here they would have surrounded the massive stone circles and the royal urns would be taken from the various lords and placed on the Green stone altar. The ceremony would be conducted, and the urns would be blessed and taken to their burial spots, which had been prepared in advance. All the urns had to be buried before the group moved on.

Once all this was done, everybody would then move up to the Great Cursus. This is a long, oblong, enclosed mound with a single stone on the east end. The alignment is exactly the same as the Heel stone's is to Stonehenge. The priests knew that this stone lined up with something and when everybody was in the Cursus they would reveal its magic. It may have been a star. When this part of the ceremony was finished, the masses would make their way back to Woodhenge. Seeing everything was done, they would have prepared to simply go back home.

As you can see, from what the scholars feel, it was likely that the ceremony taking here was for the purpose of honouring the dead. If there was a religious ceremony, then its purpose was a celebration of the dead. Stonehenge was not a place for special secret religious ceremonies for the priests, as many felt was the case. It had a real purpose, and this definitely included the participation of the population at large. It verifies that the ancestors were far more important to the people for protection than the ancient gods were.

Conclusion

The theme of this book is the mysterious druids. So, were they really that mysterious? Did they practice anything out of the ordinary that made them uniquely special, justifying the church accusing them of being demons? It appears none of it is true. Druids were a very evolved sect of people whose magic simply came from education. They observed and from their observations realized certain fundamentals. Case in point is the oak tree. Clearly it had the strongest wood of any tree, so it had the strongest meaning. The north star never moved in the sky, so it was deemed a focal point in their astronomy. Pigs and cows had the most economic value in the community, so in the oracle they symbolized wealth. The druids knew enough about nature to know certain plant-life like bark had the medicinal value of vitamin C in it, so it came to be recognized as medicine when someone was sick.

The world they lived in was barbaric and brutal. Everyone was fighting simply to make a living; thus, naturally they would regard the druids who studied the arts as special. The Bell Beaker People were, for the most part, agrarian and extremely dependent for survival upon the weather and seasons. When the Celts came along, they were a mix of agrarian and hunter-gatherer, plus extremely warlike. If the druids were going to survive – which they did, it was a matter of catering to their needs. In their very essence these cultures did not have the time to be studying the extra niceties of life. As such, they found they became dependent on the druids, who devoted all their time to the special aspects of life, like religion, medicine, and the arts. These cultures instinctively knew the druids had that little extra they needed to make life just a bit more complete than just with the everyday necessities of life. Naturally, by means of osmosis, the druids became extremely important to the community. This is not magic, this is survival.

However, when you start to go through the various aspects of what the druids came to know, it appears to be much more than being simple shamans. Further, when societies are going one step past mere existence to desiring meaning, then the wonder begins. A child looks up to the stars and asks if there are any patterns up there that could possibly have a meaning to his or her life. Imagine the excitement when the druid says yes, and then goes on to prove it. That knowledge in time becomes a threat to major political powers like the Roman Empire and the Roman Catholic Church. And thus, people are eventually persuaded into believing that druids are devil worshipers, when in reality they are nothing of the kind.

First and foremost, there's time they had to spend learning their trade. They knew what had to be learned was enormous. As such, a minimum time for education was needed—that being twenty-one years. This inspires curiosity. If it took that much time to become a white-robe druid, just how old was the institution? People like Pliny and Strabo claim they were a mature institution in 500 BC, so combine the two principles and suddenly it is not hard to believe their existence had to have spanned much further back than just 500 BC. Since the archaeologists cannot identify the shamans who proceeded the druids, then it's only logical to believe they probably existed as early as 2000 BC, and the information Caesar was given that they originated in Britain is, in fact, true.

From the enormous amount of material that was expected to be learned over the years, we can appreciate the type of person we are looking at. To be selected for the training was in itself quite a compliment. Unlike other institutions where you go and try your luck to apply for entrance; here the druids went around the country and personally chose the people (children) who could make the grades. If you were selected it spoke volumes on your educational credentials. When you consider you were only given one day to fully memorize a bardic poem, it means you had to have a disciplined mind. Because by the end of the year you were expected to know 365 more. Further, you were expected to remember them by heart for the rest of your life. As mentioned earlier, that alone means that by the time you qualified as a full druid, you would have learned 7665 poems. And remember this is the basic level too.

If what Julius Caesar wrote is true, a druid was expected to learn Greek on top of the bardic poems and to be able to conduct business in this language. Then there was Ogham, biology, astronomy, mathematics, the animal oracle, politics, bard poetry, and Brehon. A druid was expected to know the arts of all the trades below himself. Bards, for example, were the chief poets of the courts. The druid could be easily take his place if need be. It is mesmerizing when you think about it. The entire culture of a people was contained in one person. Kings like Cormac MacAirte were fully aware of this and knew the enormous importance to the country. When you think of the hundreds of druids that were killed at Mona by the Romans c. 61 AD, culturally speaking, the damage was far more than just removing life. It was the destruction of an entire race.

Next, the biggest issue is the origin of the druids. This has been a subject of enormous debate. The reason is that most people are not taking the time to do their research. They get bits of information on a subject, which many are already prejudiced on, and draw a full conclusion from it. The prevalent evidence most critics work with is that the first druid was recorded by the Greeks in 500 BC. What they do not take into consideration is that what the Greeks saw were druids of a fully developed culture. The druids did not magically appear out of thin air in 500 BC. To know what they knew obviously took some time to evolve; so people like Jean Markale, who says it's more than plausible they had to have existed previous to 500 BC, are quite sensible. As you know, he dates their origins to 800 BC. Other authors say the same thing. And that means the druids were around during the Urnfield Culture period at minimum. But when you now attach an observation made by Francis Pryor and people like William Stukeley on the druids; when there is no name for the shamans who possibly existed before the druids, then it begs the conclusion that the druids had to have been there all along. And no one is questioning the fact that as Julius Caesar said, the druids originated in Britain.

Stonehenge is probably one of the most confirming facts that the druids and no one else engineered this structure. It was Pliny who spoke extensively of the druid's mathematical skills. It was William Stukeley who actually found the measurements they used to build the stone structure. As you will recall, the fundamental measurement of the whole design was 20.9 inches. To this day, besides modern archaeologists, only the druids retained this knowledge.

It would not be fair to ignore the findings of Barry Cunliffe on how druid knowledge was passed on. He claims there was a druid revival in Brittany, France in the mid to late-eighteenth century. He argues that the new druid movement went about trying to restore much of their old knowledge. It was from that movement that many people like William Stukeley, as one example, were able to acquire the information of the druids being the architects of Stonehenge and of their astronomy awareness. The problem with this argument is the timing. William Stukeley and John Aubrey got their information about the druids from late seventeenth-century research, almost a hundred years before the new movement started. Based on the fact that there is so much knowledge that went into being a druid, it would have taken an enormous amount of time to decipher, especially the mathematics. Many of the new druids would have to have had an advanced standing in the subject if they were going to convince scholars like Stukeley and Aubrey. Clearly, on this alone, there was not enough time. The druids Stukeley and Aubrey researched originated in Britain, and as Pliny pointed out, were well established. Though many believe the druids were destroyed at Mona in 61 AD by the Romans, this was clearly not a complete event. The druids did survive.

The evidence indicating druids did survive through the ages, comes from church and historical records. People like Saint Samson and Bede the Venerable continuously mention the activities of the druids in sixth century England. Irish historical records clearly show that after the famed Council of Drumceat in AD 575, the druids continued. In northern France, records show the druids were a real thorn in the side of the churches as late as the fifteenth century. It's easy to accept that the continuity existed when Stukeley and Aubrey came along.

Overall, observation is simple. The druids did originate somewhere in Britain, and the likely time was probably around 3000 BC. Their knowledge was extensive and the twenty-one years of learning it testifies to its depth. Their threat to the modern world and the church was their knowledge and not voodoo. They did not all disappear at Mona in 61 AD. Thousands survived. What they had for magic was more for mental wellbeing than mysterious.

Does the original knowledge survive? That is certainly plausible. Since a vast majority of it came from oral tradition and still, for the most part, continues in this method, no one can be certain of the full extent. The druids chose the oral way of transmitting their knowledge for a fundamental reason—simple safety. Eating pure hemlock can be dangerous. As with a pharmaceutical, you would want a person who knows exactly how to apply it properly rather than an amateur for the correct response.

BIBLIOGRAPHY

Arkinson, R.J., *Stonehenge*, Hamilton, London 2007

Burl, Aubrey, *Megalithic Brittany*, Thomas and Hudson, London 1985

Stonehenge, Robinson, London 2006

Campbell, John, *The Masks of Gods*, Penguin, New York, 1976

Carr-Gomm, Philip & Stephanie, *Druid Animal Oracle*, Simon and Shuster, New York, 1994

Caesar, Julius, *De Bello Gaulico*, Penguin Books, New York, 1998

Clark, Graham, *Prehistoric England*, F.E. Bording, London, 1940

Delaney, Frank, *Legends of Celts*, Sterling Publishing, New York, 1942

Donoghue, Clayton N., *History of the Celts*, FriesenPress, Vancouver, 2013

Duncan, Anthony, *Celtic Mysticism*, Anness Publishing, Wales, 2000

Dunlop, Storm, *Guide to Astronomy*, Harper Collins, New York, 2015

Ellis, Peter Berresford, *The Druids*, Eardmans Publishing, Michigan, 1994

(Lady) Gregory, *Gods and Fighting Men*, Senate, London, 1902

Foster, Roy (ed), *The Oxford Illustrated History of Ireland*, Oxford University Press, 2001

Hayman, Richard, *Riddles in Stone*, Hamildon Continuum, 1996

Hawkins, Gerald. S., *Stonehenge decoded*, Doubleday Inc. New York, 1965

Heinz, Sabine, *Celtic Symbols*, Sterling, New York, 1999

Jackson, Kenneth, *A Celtic Miscellany*, Sterling, New York, 1992

James, Simon, *The World of the Celts*, Thames and Hudson, London, 1993

Livy, P., *The Early History of Rome*, Penguin Books, New York 2003

Lockyer, Norman, *The Dawn of Astronomy*, Whittlesey House, New York, 1936

MacKillop, James, *Dictionary of the Celtic Mythology*, Oxford University Press, New York, 1998

Markale, Jean, *The Druids*, Inner Tradition International, Rochester, 1999

Monroe, Douglas, *The 21 Lessons of Merlin*, Llewellyn Publications, St Paul, 1998

Murray, Collin. *The Tree Oracle*, Saint Martin's Press, New York, 1988

Myers, Brendam, C., *The Mysteries of the Druidry*, New Page Books, Franklin Lakes, 1974

Nichols, R., *The Book of Druids*, New Page Books, Toronto, 1997

Parker-Pearson, Michael, *Stonehenge: A New Understanding*, The Experiment, London, 2013

Pryor, Francis, *Britain B.C.*, Harper Collins, London, 2003

Rodgers, Nigel, *The Roman World: People and Places*, Lorenz Books, London 2005

Squire, Charles, *Mythology of the Celtic People*, Senate Publishing, London, 1912

Stewart, R.J., *Celtic Gods Celtic Goddesses*, Cassell Books, London, 1992

(Lady) Wilde, *Ancient Legends of Ireland (1898)*, Sterling Publishing, New York, 1996

CPSIA information can be obtained
at www.ICGtesting.com
Printed in the USA
LVHW041047210220
647519LV00006B/17